学做中国菜
Learn to Cook Chinese Dishes

豆品类　Bean Products

外　文　出　版　社
FOREIGN LANGUAGES PRESS

前　言

朱熙钧

倘若不是为想成为专业厨师，只是为了自家享用或偶尔飨客而学做中国菜，就无须专诚拜师学艺。中国主妇的厨艺最初几乎都是从她们的老祖母和母亲那里耳濡目染学来的；待到为人妻母之后，她们之中的一些有心人或借助菜谱用心揣摩，或与友邻切磋交流，制作出的菜馔有时竟然不逊于出自名店名厨之手。当然，在中国的家庭中，擅长烹饪的男士也不在少数，而且饭店中的名厨以男性居多。

这套《学做中国菜》丛书的编撰者都是在名店主厨的烹饪大师，为了使初学者易于入门，他们以简明的文字介绍了每一菜式的用料、刀法、制作步骤等。读者只须按所列一一去做，无须多日便可熟能生巧，举一反三，厨艺大进。

《学做中国菜》系列丛书共九册，包括水产类、肉菜类、菜蔬类、豆品类、汤菜类、冷菜类、面点类、禽蛋类和家宴类。本册为《学做中国菜》系列丛书之一，共介绍40种以豆制品为原料的菜馔的制作方法。

中国是大豆的故乡。三千年前，中国人就对大豆进行加工，制作出豆腐、百叶、豆腐干、豆腐衣等等，这是中国食品制造业对世界的一大贡献。而今以豆腐或其它豆制品为原料的菜肴，仍是中国传统菜之一，而且极其丰富多彩。

豆制品的种类极多，有水豆腐、豆腐、豆腐茸、豆腐干、百叶（千张）、豆腐皮（衣）、腐竹、油豆腐、素鸡等等。

豆制品加工过程都是先将大豆用水泡涨，冲洗干净，然后加清水研磨，过滤去渣后成豆浆。另用熟石膏粉若干用水泡开，兑入烧沸的豆浆内，使之凝固成型。

水豆腐与豆腐的区别是水豆腐中含水分多，所以极嫩，不能成型，只能在汤水中飘浮，俗称豆腐脑；而豆腐水分较少，固能成型。如果将豆浆与熟石膏粉配比稍加调整，制成豆腐后再将水分压干，就可制成豆腐干。制作豆腐干时加入不同调料，又有白干、香干、黄干、酱干等之分。

百叶的制法是在豆腐即将成型时，将其摊平用布分隔，再压干水分而成；素鸡则是用多层百叶卷起扎紧而成；若将豆腐切成块用油炸至外皮金黄、内松空即成油豆腐；待烧开的豆浆冷却以后，将凝结在豆浆表层的薄油皮逐层捞起晾干就成了一张张豆腐衣；将豆腐衣卷紧成长条就是腐竹了。将黄豆或绿豆浸泡在水中，保持适当的温度，经过三五日，就会生发出嫩芽，这便是黄豆芽和绿豆芽。

以上介绍各类豆制品，现都无需自己制作，在副食商店和超级市场内皆可购得。这里略作介绍，烹调时可根据豆腐制品不同的质地，采用相宜的方法烹调。

豆制品的烹调方法极多，丰简随意，调味从心，粗料细作，素菜荤作，荤素相配都很鲜美。烹调方法有：氽、熬、烩、炖、焖、煮、烧、炸、煸、炒、煎、烹、塌、蒸、烤、拌等等。

豆腐的烹调方法虽多，但都要在烹调前去掉豆腐中的异味。以下介绍几种去异味的方法：（一）放入开水锅中煮；（二）上笼屉蒸透；（三）用小火焖出蜂孔；（四）切成小丁用开水冲烫。

Foreword

Zhu Xijun

You don't have to take lessons from a professional teacher to learn the art of Chinese cooking if all you want to do is to entertain your friends or cook for your family. Almost without exception, Chinese women learn this skill by watching and working together with their mothers or grandmothers. After they become wives or mothers themselves, the most diligent among them will try to improve their techniques by consulting cook books and exchanging experiences with their neighbors. In this way they eventually become as skilled as the best chefs in established restaurants. It should be noted, of course, that most of the well-known chefs in famous restaurants are men because many men in Chinese homes are just as good at the art of cooking as their wives.

This book in the *Learn to Cook Chinese Dishes* series has been compiled by master chefs. They have used simple explanations to introduce the ingredients, the ways of cutting, and the cooking procedures for each Chinese recipe. Readers who follow the directions will before long become skilled in the art of Chinese cooking. The entire set consists of nine volumes, covering freshwater and seafood dishes, meat dishes, vegetable dishes, courses made from soy beans, soups, cold dishes, pastries, dishes of eggs and poultry, and recipes for family feasts. This particular volume presents forty different foods prepared with bean curd.

China is the home country of soy beans and the Chinese people began to process beans for food in the form of various types of bean curd 3,000 years ago. This has been a great contribution to the food industry of the world. Today, bean curd and other bean products remain a popular type of food in China and provide ingredients for a wide range of dishes.

Food made from beans comes in many forms including the soft bean curd, ordinary bean curd, fluffy bean curd, dried bean curd, bean curd leaves, bean curd peels, fried bean curd, dried bean curd cream in tight rolls and "meatless chicken" -- a kind of bean curd with a texture like that of chicken meat.

All bean products used for food are prepared by first soaking the beans in water. After the beans rise, wash them clean, grind them, and filter off the residue to make bean curd milk. Heat this and then soak a certain amount of editable plaster in water to mix with the boiling bean curd milk. When the mixture solidifies, bean curd is made.

Soft bean curd is distinguished from other kinds of bean curd in containing more water. It is so soft that it cannot be shaped into any solid form and has to be kept in water in a container, thus known as jellied bean curd. Ordinary bean curd has less water content. "Meatless chicken" is made by placing multiple layers of flat sheets of bean curd tightly together. When bean curd is cut into small pieces and deep-fried until it is golden yellow in color and very soft inside, it is known as fried bean curd. When boiled bean curd milk cools off, lift the layer of oily bean curd cream that forms on the top and let it dry to become bean curd peel. When bean curd peels are rolled up, they become known as dried bean curd cream in tight rolls. If soy beans or green beans are soaked in water and kept at the right temperature for three to five days, bean sprouts will grow.

None of these bean products need to be made by individual cooks at home since they are readily available in Chinese grocery stores. Different kinds of bean curd products require different kinds of cooking skills as outlined in this book.

The ways of cooking bean curd are many and easy to accomplish. They can be modified according to the desire of individual cooks. Bean curd can be prepared to look like real meat and can be given meat dish names. Bean curd dishes also make good combinations for meals with meat dishes. The basic methods for cooking bean curd dishes include quick-boiling, stewing, precooking before stewing, braising, boiling, stir-frying, quick-frying, deep-frying, deep-frying before stir-frying, raw stir-frying, steaming, and roasting.

No matter what method you employ, make sure to remove the undesirable special smell of bean curd before cooking. To achieve this, you may do the following: (1) Boil the bean curd in hot water; (2) Steam well in a steamer; (3) Simmer over a low fire; and (4) Cut the bean curd into dices and quickly run them through boiling water.

目　录
Contents

名词解释 Terms Used in Chinese Cooking

上浆: 猪肉丝、猪肉片、牛肉丝、牛肉片、羊肉丝、羊肉片、鸡肉片在烹制前都要上浆。上浆大多用于滑溜、滑炒、清炒、酱爆等烹调方法。上浆好坏，直接影响烹调出菜肴的质量。上浆就是把切好的肉，用水冲洗净，放入盐、料酒、淀粉(有时也放鸡蛋)，拌匀后，向一个方向搅拌，感到有劲为止。

Coating (*shangjiang*): Shreds and slices of pork, beef, mutton and chicken have to be coated before they are cooked in such ways as slippery-frying, quick-frying and stir-frying. And how the meat is coated has a direct bearing on the quality of the cooked dish. The coating process involves first washing the cut meat, then adding in salt, cooking wine, and cornstarch(sometimes eggs are also used) and stiring well in the same direction until you feel it is a bit sticky.

刀工 Cutting techniques:

直刀法: 就是指刀同砧板垂直的刀法，分切、剁、砍，切是一般用于无骨的主料，剁是将无骨的主料制成茸的一种刀法，砍通常用于加工带骨的或硬的主料。

Straight-cutting: Holding the knife perpendicularly over the chopping board to cut, chop and heavy-cut the main ingredient. Cutting is applied to boneless meat ingredients, chopping is done to turn boneless ingredients into pulp or paste and heavy-cutting is used when preparing meat with bones or other hard ingredients.

平刀法: 是刀面与砧板平行的一种刀法，分推刀、拉刀。推刀就是把刀从刀尖一直推到刀根，拉刀就是把刀从刀根拉到刀尖。平切就是把刀一切到底。

Horizontal-cutting: Holding the knife flat against the chopping board to push it or pull it through the ingredients.Pushing means to push the knife through the ingredients from the knife's tip through to its end while pulling involves going through the ingredients from the end to the tip of the knife.

斜刀法: 刀面同砧板面成小于 90 度夹角的刀法。

Slashing: To cut by holding the knife in an angle smaller than 90 degrees from the surface of the chopping board.

花刀: 是在主料表面用横、竖两种刀法的不同变化，切(不断)出花纹，经加热后，主料卷曲成各种形状的刀法，有菊花形花刀，麦穗刀，鳞毛形花刀等。

Mixed cutting: To cut straight and then cross with sideways cuts to produce varied patterns. When heated, the ingredients cut in this way will roll up into different forms such as chrysanthemums, wheat ears and scales, according to the ways they are cut.

片: 用切或片的方法将原料加工成薄片。质地硬的原料用切，质地软的用片的方法加工成薄片。

Slicing (*pian*):By either cutting or slicing to turn the ingredients into thin slices. Hard ingredients require cutting while soft ingredients require slicing.

丝: 丝有粗细之分，一般在0.2-0.4 厘米左右。一般先将主料切成 0.2-0.4 厘米的薄片，再将这些薄片排成瓦楞状，排叠要整齐，左手按稳主料，不可滑动，用刀把主料切成丝。

Shredding (*si*): The thickness of shreds usually varies between 0.2 (0±08 in) and 0.4 cm (0±16 in). First, either chunks of meat or vegetables are cut into thin slices of 0.2 to 0.4 cm in thickness. The slices are then arranged neatly like roof tiles.Pressed steadily underneath the left hand of the chef, the slices are finally cut into shreds.

条：条的成形方法，是先把主料切成厚片，再将片切成条，条的粗细取决于片的厚薄。

Strapping (*tiao*): Main raw materials are cut into thick slices that are cut again into straps the size of which is decided by the thickness of the slices.

粒：粒比丁小些一般在0.3厘米见方，切的方法同丁相同。

Grain-sized dicing (*li*): Cut in the same way as diced pieces, they are simply much smaller in size. The most common size is 0.3 cm (0.12 in) each side.

丁：先将主料切成厚片，再将厚片切成条，然后再切成丁。丁有大小之分，大丁在2厘米见方，小丁在1厘米见方。

Dicing (*ding*): Main raw materials are cut into thick slices that are cut into straps. In turn, the straps are reduced to diced pieces that may be as large as 2 cm (0.8in) on each side or as small as 1 cm (0.39 in) on each side.

末：末比粒还小，将丁或粒剁碎就可以了。

Mincing (*mo*): Ground ingredients are even smaller than grain-sized dices.Usually the diced pieces are chopped into mince.

茸：用排剁的方法把主料剁得比末还细。

Chopping to make a pulp (*rong*): To chop the materials, knife cut after knife cut into pieces even finer than minced materials.

块：块是采用切、砍、剁等刀法加工而成的。块分菱形块、方块、长方块、滚刀块等。

Cutting into chunks (*kuai*): Chunks are the result of perpendicular and sideways cutting as well as chopping. The chunks come in many shapes such as diamonds, squares and rectangles.

炸：是旺火加热，以食油为传热介质烹调方法，特点是火旺用油量多。

Deep-frying (*zha*): Heat the cooking oil over a hot fire and deep-fry the materials. This process is characterized by a hot fire and a large amount of oil.

炒：炒是将加工成丁、丝、条、球等小型主料投入油锅中，在旺火上急速翻炒成熟的一种烹调方法。炒分滑炒、熟炒、干炒等几种。滑炒是经过粗加工的小型主料先经上浆，再用少量油在旺火上急速翻炒，最后以湿淀粉勾芡的方法，叫滑炒。熟炒是把经过初步加工后的半成品，改切成片或块，不上浆，用旺火烧锅热油，放入半成品翻炒，再加佐料而成。煸炒和干炒是把主料煸一下，在热油锅急火炒至退水后，加佐料，起锅。

Stir-frying (*chao*): Put processed materials in the shape of diced pieces, shreds, straps, or balls into the heated oil and quickly stir them over a hot fire. There are several different ways of stir-frying. *Hua chao* (stir-frying with batter), for example, requires that the ingredients are put in a batter and then quickly stirred in a small quantity of oil over a hot fire.The final process is to apply the mixture of cornstarch and water. *Shu chao* (stir-frying precooked food) does not require that the materials be put into some kind of batter. Simply put the precooked materials into the wok and use a hot fire before adding spicing agents. *Bian chao* and *gan chao* (raw stir-frying) calls for the simmering of main ingredients, then quick-stir-frying over a hot fire until the juice is fully absorbed. Now add spicing agents and the dish is ready to serve.

溜：溜是先将主料用炸的方法加热成熟，然后把调制好的卤汁浇淋于主料上，或将主料投入卤汁中搅拌的一种烹调方法。
Slippery-frying(*liu*): First deep-fry the main ingredient and then top it with sauce or mix the main ingredient in the sauce.

爆：爆是将脆性主料投入适量的油锅中，用旺火高油温快速加热的一种烹调方法。
Quick-fry over high heat (*bao*): Put crispy materials into the wok with medium amount of oil and quickly stir the materials over high heat.

隔水炖：隔水加热使主料成熟的方法，叫做隔水炖。
Steaming in a container (*ge shui dun*): Put the main ingredient into a bowl or similar container and cook it in a steamer.

烧：烧是经过炸、煎、煸炒或水煮的主料，再用葱姜炝锅后，倒入翻炒，然后加适量汤水和调味品，用旺火烧开，中小火烧透入味，改用旺火使卤汁稠浓的一种烹调方法。
Stewing over medium,then high heat (*shao*): After putting scallions and ginger into the wok, put in the main materials that have been deep-fried, or stir-fried or boiled and stirred. Then add water and seasoning materials to cook over a hot fire until the ingredients boil. Turn the fire to medium or low to allow full absorption of the sauce into the ingredients before turning the fire hot again to thicken the sauce.

扒：扒是将经过初步熟处理的主料整齐地排放在锅内，加汤汁和调味品，用旺火烧开，小火烧透入味，出锅前，原汁勾芡的一种烹调方法。
Stewing and adding thickening (*pa*): Neatly arrange the main ingredient that has already been cooked,add water and flavoring materials and cook over a hot fire until it boils. Turn the fire to low to allow full absorption of the flavor. Thicken the sauce with the mixture of water and cornstarch before bringing the dish out of the wok to serve.

煮：煮是将主料放入多量的汤汁或水中，先用旺火煮沸，再用中小火烧熟的一种烹调方法。
Boiling (*zhu*): Put main materials of the dish into the wok with an adequate amount of water and cook it over a hot fire to the boiling point. Then continue to cook after turning the fire to low or medium.

烩：将加工成片、丝、条、丁等料的多种主料放在一起，烩锅翻炒后，用旺火制成半汤半菜的菜肴，这种烹调方法就是烩。
Precooking and then stewing (*hui*): First heat the oil in the wok, put in scallions and ginger and then put several kinds of main ingredients that have been cut into slices, shreds, chunks or dices to cook over a hot fire so as to create a dish of half soup and half vegetables and meat.

煎：煎是以少量油布遍锅底、用小火将主料煎熟使两面呈黄色的烹调方法。

Sauteing (*jian*): Put a small amount of oil into the wok and use a low fire to cook the main ingredient until it is golden brown on both sides.

蒸：蒸是以蒸汽的热力使经过调味的主料成熟或酥烂入味的烹调方法。

Steaming (*zheng*): Cook the materials that have already been prepared with flavoring agents by using hot steam.

拔丝：拔丝又叫拉丝，是将经过油炸的小型主料，挂上能拔出丝来的糖浆的一种烹调方法。

Crisp frying with syrup (*ba si*): Put small-size ingredients that have already been deep-fried into sugar syrup heated in the wok. When diners pick up the materials, long sugar threads are created.

焯水：就是把经过初加工的主料，放在水锅中加热至沸(主要为去腥味或异味)，原料出水后供烹调菜肴之用。焯水分冷水锅和热水锅。冷水锅就是主料与冷水同时下锅，水沸取出，适用于腥气重血量多的主料如牛肉、羊肉等。热水锅就是先将锅中水加热至沸，再将主料下锅，翻滚后再取出主料。适用于腥气小，血污少的主料如鸡、鸭、猪肉和蔬菜。

Quick boiling (*chao*): Put main ingredients into the pot and heat the water to boiling point(in order to remove fishy or other undesirable smells). Then cook the boiled ingredients. The quick-boiling process includes cold water boiling and hot water boiling. The former requires putting the ingredients into the pot toge ther with the cold water and then taking them out when the water boils. This process is often applied to such materials as beef and mutton,which contain a fishy smell and a lot of blood. The latter calls for heating the water in the pot to boiling point before putting the ingredients in.This is applicable to materials like chicken, duck, pork and vegetables that have a much weaker fishy smell and less blood.

油温表

油温类型	俗　称	油温特点
温油锅	四成 70℃－100℃	无青烟，无响声，油面平静。
热油锅	五、六成热 110℃－170℃	微有青烟，油四周向内翻动。
旺油锅	七、八成热 180℃－220℃	有青烟，油面仍较平静，用勺搅动有响声。

Temperatures of cooking oil:

Category	Temperature	Features
Luke-warm	70°C－100°C 158°F-212°F	Smokeless, soundless, calm oil surface
Hot oil	110°C－170°C 230°F-338°F	Slight smoke, oil stirs from the side to the center of the wok
Very hot oil	180°C－220°C 356°F-428°F	Smokes, the surface remains calm and when stirred, sizzling sound is heard.

花椒：花椒是花椒树的果实，以籽小，壳厚紫色为好。味香麻，烹调肉类的调料。

Prickly ash (*hua jiao*): Seeds from prickly ash trees, which are small and light purple in color. They have a slight effect of numbness on the tongue. Used to cook dishes with meat.

椒盐：味香麻，是炸菜蘸食的调味品。把花椒和盐按1:3的比例在锅中，微火炒成焦黄，磨成细末，即成。

Pepper salt (*jiao yan*): This mixture is made by stirring one portion of peppercorns and three portions of salt in the wok until they turn crispy yellowish in color and release their fragrance. Then finely grind the mixture into powder. It serves as a seasoning for deep-fried dishes.

味精：根据个人口味，也可不放味精，而使用适量的鸡精。
Monosodium glutamate and chicken bouillon: Though MSG is essential in traditional Chinese cooking, for many who do not find it agreeable, chicken bouillon can be used instead.

茴香：小茴香是茴香菜的籽，呈灰色，似稻粒，有浓郁的香味。
Fennel seeds (*hui xiang*): Seeds of fennel plants, grey in color and similar to unhusked rice grains in shape, have a hot flavor.

大茴香：又名八角、大料，形如星状，味甜浓，烹调肉类的调料。
Star anise (*da hui xiang*): In the shape of stars, they have a strong and sweet flavor. Mostly used in cooking meat dishes.

糟：制作料酒剩下的酒糟经过加工就成为烹调用的糟，糟具有同料酒同样的调味作用。
Steaming with distillers'grains sauce (*zao*): Distillers'grains, which are left over from liquor making, are processed into a spicy agent for cooking that has the same function as the cooking wine.

五香料：大料、茴香、桂皮、甘草、丁香(丁香花蕾)五种香料

混合为五香料，研成粉为五香粉。
Five Spices (*wu xiang liao*): A mixture of powdered star anise, fennel seed, cinnamon bark, licorice root and clove buds. Also referred to as the "five-powdered spices".

桂皮：是桂树的皮，外皮粗糙呈现褐色。
Cinnamon (*gui pi*): The bark of cinnamon trees, brown in color.

料酒：常用料酒是用糯米等粮食酿制成的，料酒，在烹调菜肴过程中起去腥、增香的作用，特别是烹制水产或肉类时少不了它。如没有料酒，可用适量的啤酒或白兰地代替，但没有料酒好。
Cooking wine (*liao jiu*): Cooking wine, brewed from grain, is applied to remove the fishy smell and increase the aroma of the dish. It is particularly essential when cooking dishes with aquatic ingredients and meat. While cooking wine is most desirable, in its absence, beer and brandy can be used.

勾芡：勾芡就是在菜肴接近成熟时，将调好的湿淀粉加入锅内，搅拌均匀，使卤汁稠浓。增加卤汁对主料的附着力的一种方法。
Thickening with mixture of cornstarch and water (*gou qian*): When the dish is nearly cooked, put a previously prepared mixture

of cornstarch and water into the dish and stir well so as to thicken the sauce or broth. This process promotes the flavored sauce to stay with the main materials of the dish.

勾芡作用： 1、增加菜肴汤汁的粘性和浓度。2、增加菜肴的光泽。

Major functions of this process: (1) Increase the stickiness and thickness of the sauce of the dish. (2) Making the dish look more shiny.

勾芡关键： 1、勾芡必须在菜肴即将成熟时候进行。2、勾芡时锅中汤汁不可太多或太少。3、必须在菜肴的口味、颜色已经调准后进行。4、勾芡时锅中油不宜太多。

Key for using this process: (1) This process must be conducted when the cooking of the dish is nearly complete. (2) The sauce in the wok must not be too much or too little when this thickening technique is applied. (3) This process can only be done after all efforts for flavoring and coloring of the dish are completed. (4) When doing the thickening process, the wok should not have too much oil in it.

如何使用筷子

吃中式饭菜一般使用筷子。筷子是用木或竹、骨及其它材料制成长25-30厘米、上方（各边为8毫米）下圆（直径为3-5毫米）的二根小棍。

使用时须依靠拇指及食指、中指和无名指的连贯配合。方法是：首先把两根筷子拿在右手，用食指、中指及无名指在距筷子近上端处各夹一根筷子，再把拇指和食指合在一起，如图1。用筷子取食时，把食指和中指夹的一根向上抬，另一根不动，使两根筷子张开。如图2。夹取食物时，把食指和中指夹的筷子往下压，夹住食物，抬起筷子进食，如图3。

How to Use Chopsticks

Chopsticks for eating Chinese food are usually made from wood, bamboo, animal bones or other materials. About 25 to 30

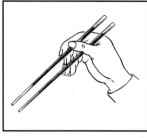

(1)

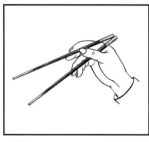

(2)

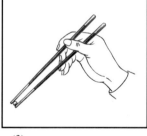

(3)

centimeters long, their top is square, about 0.8 square centimeter, and the low end round with a diameter of 3 to 5 millimeters.

The correct way of using the chopsticks requires concerted efforts of the thumb, index finger, middle finger and third finger. Hold the pair of chopsticks in the right hand, using the index finger, middle and third fingers to keep the chopsticks steady near their top and then push them open by moving the thumb and index finger. (See Drawing 1)

To pick things up with chopsticks, lift upward one of the two chopsticks with the index and middle fingers while keeping the other one where it is so as to separate the two. (See Drawing 2)

Once the chopsticks have picked up the food, press one of the chopsticks with the thumb and index finger and raise the pair. (See Drawing 3)

笼屉　蒸锅
Steaming tray(*long ti*)Usually made of bamboo or wood, these often come in several tiers

炒锅
Skillet

火锅
Hot-pot

砂锅
Earthen pot

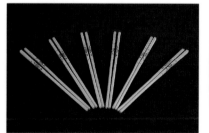

汤勺　炒铲　漏勺
Soup spoon Shovel Perforated spoon

筷子
Chopsticks

菜（面）板
Chopping board

麻辣豆腐

主料：豆腐 500 克

辅料：嫩牛肉 150 克

调料：四川郫县豆瓣酱 50 克、豆豉 2 克、干红辣椒 10 克、青蒜 75 克、花椒粉 2 克、姜末 3 克、酱油 10 克、料酒 10 克、盐 2 克、味精 2 克、鸡汤 200 克、湿淀粉 10 克、花生油 75 克

制作：①将豆腐切成 3 厘米见方的块，投入沸水中焯烫，捞出滤去水分。

②嫩牛肉切长、宽、厚皆约 0.3 厘米的粒，干红辣椒洗净去蒂、籽同青蒜都切成 0.6 厘米长的段。

③炒锅置中火上加花生油烧至七成热，下牛肉粒煵炒至酥香，烹入料酒，下豆瓣酱、豆豉，煵出香味，然后加红辣椒和姜末，炒匀后加鸡汤，再放入豆腐、酱油、盐、烧沸转小火。烧透入味，加味精，用湿淀粉勾芡，下青蒜出锅，撒上花椒粉即可。

特点：开胃爽口

口味：辣麻鲜香

Spicy Bean Curd

Ingredients：

500 grams (1.1 lb) bean curd
150 grams (0.33 lb) tender beef
50 grams (0.11 lb) soy bean paste
2 grams (1/2 tsp) black bean paste
10 grams (1/3 oz) dried red chili
75 grams (2 1/2 oz) garlic leaves
2 grams (1/2 tsp) Chinese prickly ash powder
3 grams (1/10 oz) chopped ginger
10 grams (1 1/2 tsp) soy sauce
10 grams (2 tsp) cooking wine
2 grams (1/3 tsp) salt
2 grams (1/2 tsp) MSG
200 grams (2/5 cup) chicken soup
10 grams (2 tsp) mixture of cornstarch and water
75 grams (5 1/2 tbsp) cooking oil

Directions：

1. Cut the bean curd into dices 3 cm (1.2 inches) long on each side. Quick-boil and take out to drain off the water.

2. Cut the tender beef into dices 0.3 cm (0.12 inch) long on each side. Cut the red chili into sections 0.6 cm (0.24 inch) long. Cut the garlic leaves into sections of the same length.

3. Heat the oil in a wok to 180-200℃ (355-390°F) and stir-fry the beef dices until they produce a distinctive aroma. Add the cooking wine, soy bean paste and black bean paste until there is a clear aromatic smell. Add the red chili and ginger. Stir to mix well. Add the chicken soup, bean curd, soy sauce and salt, and bring to a boil. Turn to a low fire to simmer. Before the soup is all gone, add the MSG. Thicken the remaining soup with the mixture of cornstarch and water. Add the sectioned garlic leaves and sprinkle on the powder of Chinese prickly ash. Now it is ready to serve.

Features：Very appetizing.
Taste：Spicy and delicious.

麻辣豆腐
Spicy Bean Curd

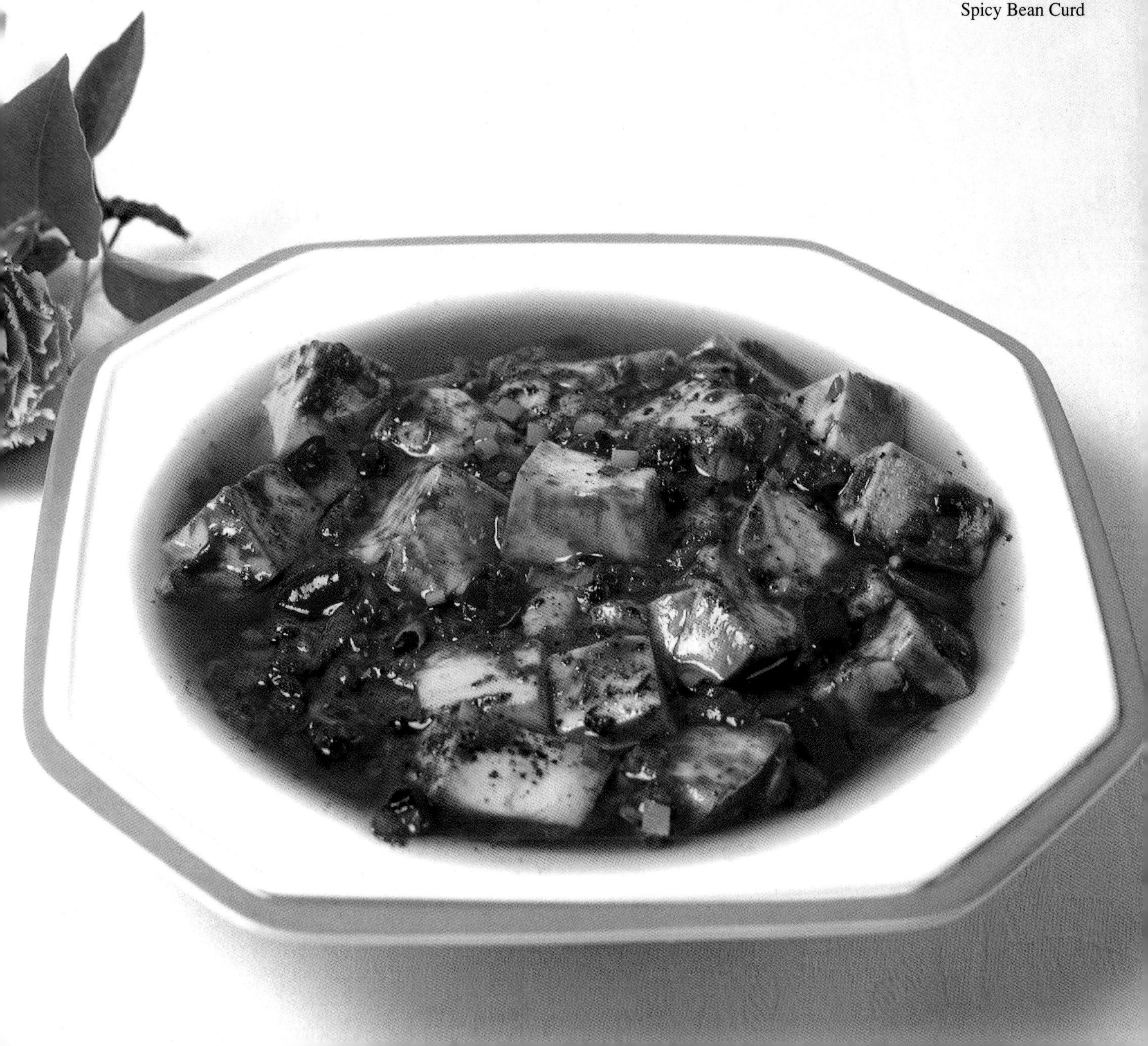

葱辣豆腐

主料：豆腐 300 克

辅料：大葱 50 克、红干辣椒 5 只

调料：酱油 25 克、料酒 5 克、味精 1 克、花生油 400 克（实耗 100 克）、鸡汤 175 克、盐 1 克

制作：①将豆腐切成长 5 厘米、宽 2.5 厘米、厚 1 厘米的长方块，用洁布吸去表面水分。大葱切成长 5 厘米的段。辣椒洗净去蒂、籽，切成细丝。

②炒锅烧热，放油烧至七成热，分批投入豆腐炸至金黄色，倒出沥油。锅中留油 25 克，放辣椒煸出香味，再下葱段、料酒，爆出香味，下豆腐、酱油、盐、鸡汤，加盖焖 15 分钟，放入味精调好味，装深盘即可。

特点：色泽黄亮，葱香浓郁

口味：香辣咸鲜

Bean Curd with Chili and Scallions

Ingredients：
300 grams (0.66 lb) bean curd
50 grams (0.11 lb) scallions
5 dried red chilies
25 grams (1 1/2 tbsp) soy sauce
5 grams (1 tsp) cooking wine
1 gram (1/4 tsp) MSG
1 gram (1/6 tsp) salt
400 grams (4/5 cup) oil (only 100 g or 7 tbsp to be consumed)
175 grams (12 tbsp) chicken soup

Directions：
1. Cut the bean curd into chunks 5 cm (2 inches) long, 2.5 cm (1 inch) wide and 1 cm (0.4 inch) thick. Use a piece of dry cloth to absorb the water on the surface of the bean curd. Cut the scallions into sections 5 cm (2 inches) long. Remove the stems and seeds of the red chilies and cut into small shreds.

2. Heat the oil in a wok to 180-200℃ (355-390°F) and put in the bean curd chunks to deep-fry until they are golden yellow in color. Take out and drain off the oil. Keep 25 g (1 2/3 tbsp) of oil in the wok and stir-fry the chili shreds until they produce a distinctive aroma. Add the scallions and cooking wine. When these produce their aroma, add the deep-fried bean curd, soy sauce, salt and chicken soup, and put on the wok cover to simmer for 15 minutes. Add the MSG and the dish is ready to serve.

Features：Golden yellow in color, the dish has a strong aroma from the scallions.
Taste：Spicy, salty and delicious.

葱辣豆腐
Bean Curd with Chili and Scallions

锅塌豆腐

主料：豆腐 200 克

辅料：鸡蛋 2 只、面粉 50 克

调料：料酒 10 克、盐 3 克、味精 1 克、葱末 3 克、姜末 5 克、麻油 10 克、鸡汤 75 克、油 100 克

制作：①将豆腐切成长 4 厘米、宽 2.5 厘米、厚 0.4 厘米的片，平放在盘内，撒上葱姜末各 2 克、盐 1 克、料酒 5 克，腌片刻。鸡蛋磕破将蛋液放入碗中打散。

②炒锅烧热，下油烧至七成热时先将豆腐两面均匀蘸上面粉，再下鸡蛋液裹匀，逐片投入油锅中，煎至两面金黄，再投入葱姜末、料酒、鸡汤、盐、味精烧沸后加盖转小火烧 5 分钟至汤汁收干，淋上麻油出锅。

特点：色泽金黄，外脆内嫩

口味：香醇

Slow-stewed Bean Curd with Chicken Soup

Ingredients：
200 grams (0.44 lb) bean curd
2 eggs
50 grams (0.11 lb) wheat flour
10 grams (2 tsp) cooking wine
3 grams (1/2 tsp) salt
1 gram (1/4 tsp) MSG
3 grams (1/10 oz) finely cut scallions
5 grams (1/6 oz) chopped ginger
10 grams (2 tsp) sesame oil
75 grams (5 tbsp) chicken soup
100 grams (7 tbsp) cooking oil

Directions：
1. Cut the bean curd into slices 4 cm (1.6 inches) long, 2.5 cm (1 inch) wide and 0.4 cm (0.16 inch) thick. Put them on a plate and sprinkle on the scallion and ginger 2 g (1/15 oz) each. Add 1g(1/6tsp) of the salt, and 5 g(1tsp)of the cooking wine to marinate.

2. Heat the oil in a wok to 180-200℃ (355-390˚F). Whip the eggs and dip the cut bean curd slices to allow them to be evenly covered with the whipped egg. Deep-fry the bean curd slices until they are golden yellow on both sides. Add the ginger, scallions, chicken soup, the remaining cooking wine and salt, MSG, and when mixture starts to boil, cover the wok lid. Turn to a low fire and cook until the soup is absorbed. Sprinkle on the sesame oil and bring out to serve.

Features：Golden yellow in color, the bean curd is crispy outside and tender inside.
Taste：Simply delicious.

锅塌豆腐
Slow-stewed Bean Curd with Chicken Soup

宫保豆腐

主料：豆腐 300 克

辅料：猪肉酱 100 克、花生仁 50 克

调料：泡制辣椒 15 克、葱末和姜末各 5 克、豆瓣酱 15 克、酱油 10 克、糖 2 克、盐 2 克、味精 1 克、香醋 5 克、料酒 10 克、鸡汤 150 克、湿淀粉 10 克、花椒粉 1 克、油 750 克（实耗 100 克）。

制作：①花生仁用水泡软、去衣，沥干水分用低温油炸熟。

②将豆腐切成 2.5 厘米见方的块，入沸水焯后捞出冷却。

③炒锅烧热，下油烧至七成热，分批下豆腐炸成金黄色倒出沥油。

④原锅留油 25 克烧热，下辣椒炒至深红色，加葱姜末、猪肉酱、豆瓣酱煸炒出香味，烹料酒，下豆腐、鸡汤、酱油、盐、糖焖烧 5 分钟，加味精调味，用湿淀粉勾芡，倒入熟花生仁，烹香醋撒上花椒粉出锅。

特点：风味浓厚

口味：麻辣鲜香

Quick-stir-fried Bean Curd with Chili & Peanuts

Ingredients：

300 grams (0.66 lb) bean curd
100 grams (0.22 lb) minced pork
50 grams (0.11 lb) peanuts
15 grams (1/2 oz) dried red chili, previously soaked in water
5 grams (1/6 oz) finely cut scallions
5 grams (1/6 oz) chopped ginger
15 grams (1 3/4 tsp) soy bean paste
10 grams (1 1/2 tsp) soy sauce
2 grams (1/3 tsp) salt
2 grams (1/2 tsp) sugar
1 gram (1/4 tsp) MSG
5 grams (1 tsp) vinegar
10 grams (2 tsp) cooking wine
150 grams (10 tbsp) chicken soup
10 grams (1 1/2 tsp) mixture of cornstarch and water
1 gram (1/5 tsp) Chinese prickly ash powder
750 grams (1 1/2 cup) oil (only 100 g or 7 tbsp to be consumed)

Directions：

1. Soak the peanuts in water to make them soft. Remove the peanut skin, drain off the water, and deep-fry them in low-temperature oil.

2. Cut the bean curd into dices 2.5 cm (1 inch) long each side, quick-boil them, drain off the water and let them cool off.

3. Heat the oil to 180-200℃ (355-390°F) and deep-fry the bean curd dices batch by batch until they are golden yellow. Take out and drain off the oil.

4. Keep 25 g (1 2/3 tbsp) of oil in the wok. Stir-fry the red chilies until they are dark red. Add the ingredients in the order of scallions, ginger, minced meat and soy bean paste, and stir-fry until they produce a strong aroma. Add ingredients in the order of cooking wine, deep-fried bean curd dices, chicken soup, soy sauce, salt and sugar, and simmer for 5 minutes. Put in the MSG and thicken the dish with the mixture of cornstarch and water. Add the fried peanuts, sprinkle on the vinegar and Chinese prickly ash powder. Take out to serve.

Features：Richly flavored.
Taste: Spicy and delicious with a strong touch of Chinese prickly ash.

宫保豆腐
Quick-stir-fried Bean Curd with Chili & Peanuts

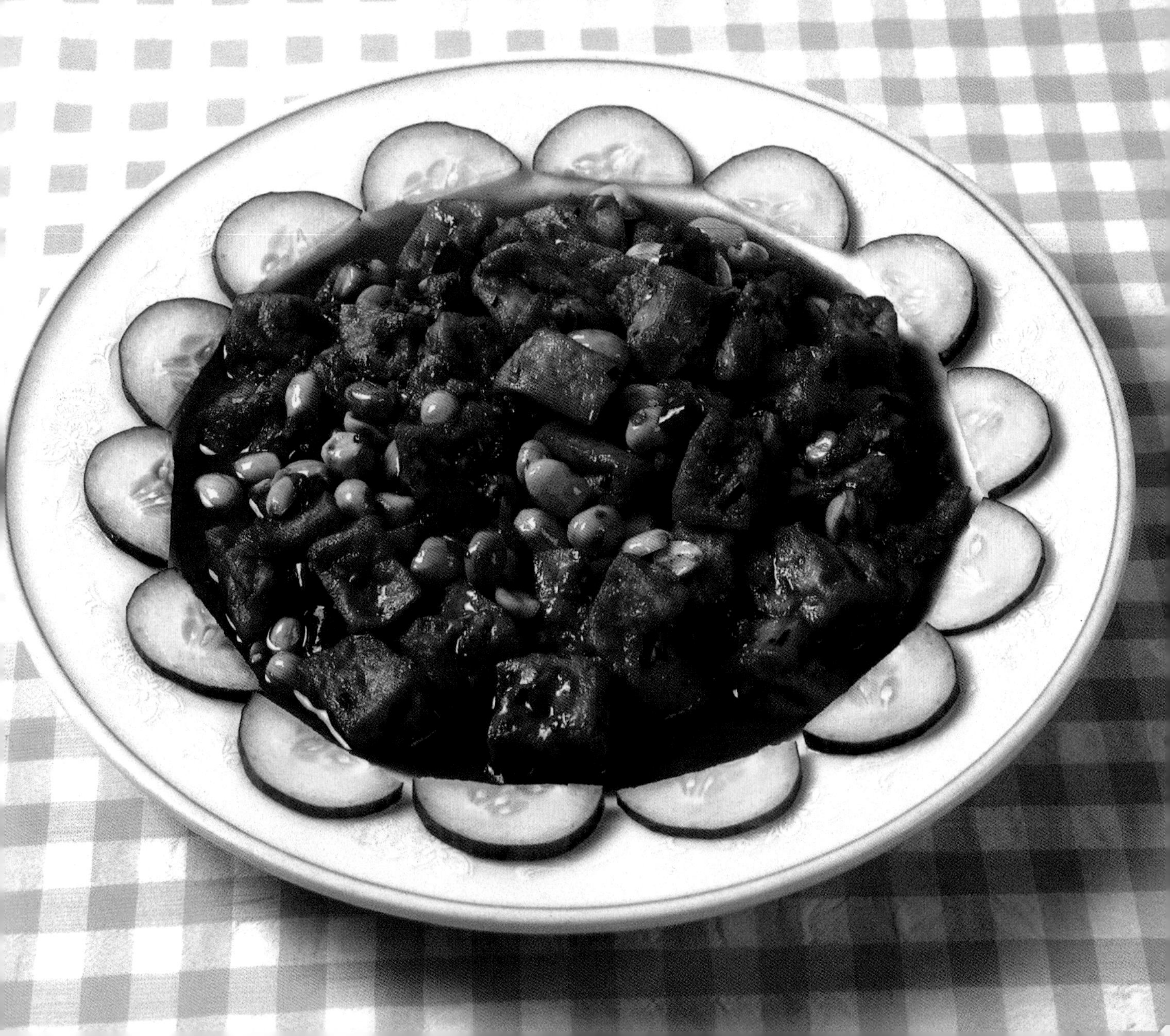

蘑菇豆腐

主料：豆腐 200 克

辅料：鲜蘑菇 100 克（或罐装蘑菇）

调料：鸡汤 100 克、酱油 5 克、糖 10 克、盐 2 克、味精 1 克、葱花 5 克、湿淀粉 15 克、料酒 10 克、油 50 克

制作：①将豆腐切成 2.5 厘米见方的块，入沸水锅焯后倒出沥干水分，鲜蘑菇洗净。

②炒锅烧热，下油烧至四成热，下葱花爆出香味，加料酒、酱油、盐、糖、鸡汤，然后倒下豆腐和鲜蘑菇大火烧开再转小火烧 5 分钟，出锅前转大火，下味精，收干汤汁，用湿淀粉勾芡。

特点：色泽红润，味鲜质嫩

口味：鲜美可口

Bean Curd with Mushrooms

Ingredients：
200 grams (0.44 lb) bean curd
100 grams (0.22 lb) fresh or canned mushrooms
100 grams (6 tbsp) chicken soup
5 grams (1 tsp) soy sauce
10 grams (2 tsp) sugar
2 grams (1/3 tsp) salt
1 gram (1/4 tsp) MSG
5 grams (1/6 oz) finely cut scallions
15 grams (1 3/4 tsp) mixture of cornstarch and water
10 grams (2 tsp) cooking wine
50 grams (3 1/2 tbsp) cooking oil

Directions：

1. Cut the bean curd into dices 2.5 cm (1 inch) long on each side. Quickly boil these and drain off the water.

2. Heat the oil to 70-100℃ (160-210°F) and stir-fry the scallions until they produce a distinctive aroma. Add the cooking wine, soy sauce, salt, sugar, soup, and then the bean curd cubes and fresh mushrooms. Use a strong fire to bring to a boil. Turn to low fire to simmer for 5 minutes. Turn to a strong fire again to boil off some of the soup. Add the MSG and the mixture of cornstarch and water to thicken the sauce.

Features：Brownish in color and tenderly delicious.
Taste：Refreshing and tasty.

蘑菇豆腐
Bean Curd with Mushrooms

三鲜豆腐

主料：豆腐 500 克

辅料：火腿 50 克、鲜蘑菇 25 克、鸡胸脯肉 50 克

调料：葱花 10 克、青椒一只、胡椒粉 1 克、盐 2 克、味精 1 克、鸡汤 250 克、麻油 5 克、色拉油 50 克、料酒 10 克、湿淀粉 10 克

制作：①将豆腐切成长 2.5 厘米、宽 2 厘米、厚 0.7 厘米的片，入沸水中焯后，再用清水漂清。青椒去蒂、籽，洗净。

②火腿、鸡胸脯肉、鲜蘑菇煮熟后切片，青椒也切片。

③炒锅烧热，下色拉油烧至五成热，下火腿片、蘑菇片、鸡肉片、青椒片翻炒数下，下料酒、鸡汤、盐、豆腐片，烧沸后转小火下胡椒粉、味精调味，然后用湿淀粉勾芡，撒上葱花，淋上麻油出锅。

特点：醇厚味美

口味：鲜嫩可口

Three-flavored Bean Curd

Ingredients：

500 grams (1.1 lb) bean curd
50 grams (0.11 lb) ham
25 grams (5/6 oz) fresh mushroom
50 grams (0.11 lb) chicken breast
10 grams (1/3 oz) finely cut scallions
1 green pepper
1 gram (1/5 tsp) pepper powder
2 grams (1/3 tsp) salt
1 gram (1/4 tsp) MSG
250 grams (1/2 cup) chicken soup
5 grams (1 tsp) sesame oil
50 grams (3 1/2 tbsp) salad oil
10 grams (2 tsp) cooking wine
10 grams (1 1/2 tsp) mixture of cornstarch and water

Directions：

1. Cut the bean curd into slices 2.5 cm (1 inch) long, 2 cm (0.8 inch) wide and 0.7 cm (0.28 inch) thick. Quick-boil these and then run them through in cold water. Remove the stem and seeds of the green pepper and wash it clean.

2. Cut the ham, chicken breast, mushrooms and green pepper into slices of similar thickness to the bean curd.

3. Heat the oil in a wok to 110-135℃ (230-275˚F). Add the slices of ham, mushrooms, chicken and green pepper, and turn over several times. Add the cooking wine, chicken soup, salt and bean curd, and bring to a boil. Turn to a low fire and add the pepper powder and MSG. Thicken the sauce with the mixture of cornstarch and water. Sprinkle on the scallions and sesame oil and the dish is ready.

Features：Richly flavored.
Taste：Refreshing and tenderly delicious.

三鲜豆腐
Three-flavored Bean Curd

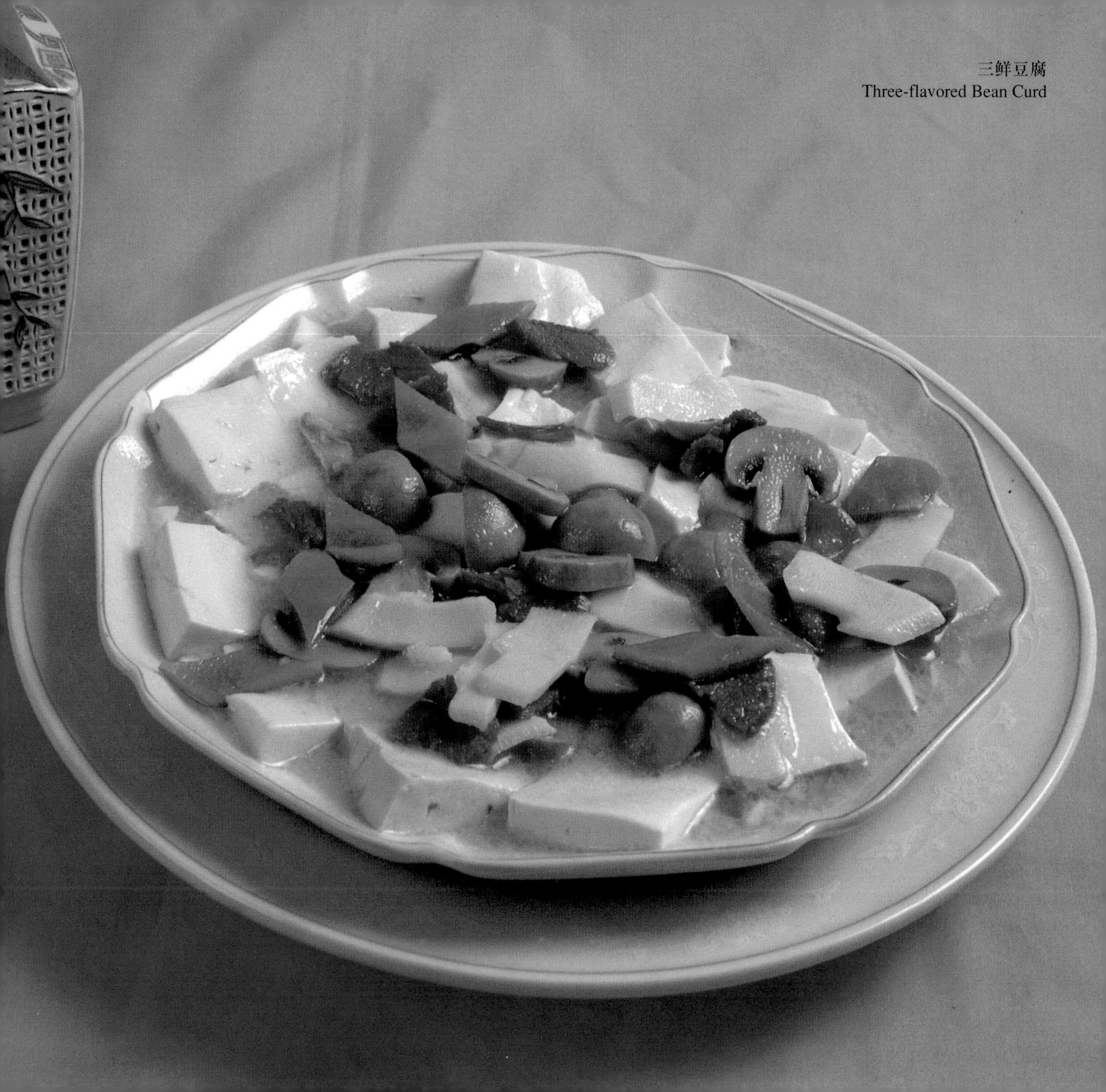

家常豆腐

主料：豆腐 400 克

辅料：鲜蘑菇 10 克（或罐装蘑菇）、冬笋 10 克、青椒一只、猪里脊肉 25 克、虾籽 0.5 克

调料：酱油 20 克、糖 5 克、料酒 5 克、蒜泥 5 克、辣油 3 克、味精 1 克、胡椒粉 1.5 克、湿淀粉 10 克、油 500 克（实耗 100 克）、鸡汤 250 克

制作：①将豆腐切成 6 厘米见方，0.7 厘米厚的块，然后再对角切成三角形，入沸水锅焯后捞起待用。青椒去蒂、籽洗净。

②蘑菇切片，冬笋、青椒、猪里脊肉分别切 6 厘米长、3 厘米宽的片。

③炒锅烧热，放油大火烧热，投入豆腐炸至金黄色捞起沥油。锅内留油 50 克，下蒜泥、肉片翻炒，再放青椒、蘑菇、笋片翻炒，放豆腐、料酒、虾籽、酱油、糖、胡椒粉、鸡汤开大火烧沸后转小火焖 5 分钟，再转大火收干汤汁，下味精、辣油调味，用湿淀粉勾芡即可。

特点：色泽桔红，香气四溢

口味：鲜香咸辣

Home-style Bean Curd

Ingredients：
400 grams (0.88 lb) bean curd
10 grams (1/3 oz) fresh or canned mushrooms
10 grams (1/3 oz) winter bamboo shoots
1 green pepper
25 grams (5/6 oz) pork tenderloin
20 grams (1 tbsp) soy sauce
5 grams (1 tsp) sugar
5 grams (1 tsp) cooking wine
5 grams (1/6 oz) mashed garlic
3 grams (3/5 tsp) spicy oil
1 gram (1/4 tsp) MSG
1 1/2 gram (1/3 tsp) pepper powder
10 grams (1 1/2 tsp) mixture of cornstarch and water
500 grams (1 cup) oil (only 1/5 to be consumed)
250 grams (1/2 cup) chicken soup

Directions：
1. Cut the bean curd into slices 6 cm (2.4 inches) long and wide and 0.7 cm (0.28 inch) thick, and cut the slices again into triangle shapes. Remove the stem and seeds of the green pepper and wash it clean.

2. Cut the bamboo shoots, mushrooms, green pepper and pork tenderloin into slices 6 cm (2.4 inches) long and 3 cm (1.2 inches) wide.

3. Heat the oil to 180-200℃ (355-390°F) and deep-fry the bean curd slices until they are golden yellow. Take out and drain off the oil. Keep 50 g (3 1/2 tbsp) oil in the wok. Add the mashed garlic and pork slices to stir-fry for 1 minute. Add the slices of green pepper, mushrooms and bamboo shoots and turn over several times. Put in the bean curd, cooking wine, soy sauce, sugar, pepper powder and chicken soup. Bring to a boil over a strong fire and turn to a low fire to simmer for 5 minutes. Turn strong fire again to reduce the sauce. Add the MSG and spicy oil and then thicken the sauce with the mixture of cornstarch and water. Sprinkle on the sesame oil and the dish is ready.

Features：Orange red in color, the dish gives off a strong, fragrant aroma.
Taste：Salty, spicy and delicious.

烤豆腐

主料：豆腐 500 克

辅料：海米 25 克

调料：花椒粉 0.5 克、酱油 5 克、味精 1 克、盐 2 克、料酒 5 克、油 25 克、蒜泥 5 克

制作：①将豆腐切成 5 厘米见方、1 厘米厚的片若干块，然后用酱油、盐、味精、料酒调和成汁均匀涂在豆腐的两面；将海米用水泡软，切成末。

②取烤盘 1 只，倒油 15 克，然后将半数的豆腐置盘中，在每块豆腐上撒上海米、蒜泥，再将另一半豆腐一一扣合在上面，将余下的油烧在豆腐上。

③将烤盘入烤箱内，先用旺火烤 5 分钟，再转中火烤 15—20 分钟，取出撒上花椒粉即可。

特点：软糯润滑，香味四溢

口味：咸香味醇

Roast Bean Curd

Ingredients：
500 grams (1.1 lb) bean curd
25 grams (5/6 oz) dried shrimps
1/2 gram (1/10 tsp) Chinese prickly ash powder
5 grams (1 tsp) soy sauce
1 gram (1/4 tsp) MSG
2 grams (1/3 tsp) salt
5 grams (1/6 oz) mashed garlic
5 grams (1 tsp) cooking wine
25 grams (1 2/3 tbsp) cooking oil

Directions：
1. Cut the bean curd into slices 5 cm (2 inches) long and wide and 1 cm (0.4 inch) thick. Rub the slices with the mixture of soy sauce, salt, MSG and cooking wine. Soak the dried shrimps in water and then chop them finely.

2. Put 15 g (1 tbsp) of oil on a roasting plate. Place half of the bean curd slices on the plate, spread chopped shrimps and mashed garlic on each slice of bean curd and cover these slices with the rest of the bean curd to make sandwich-like slices. Sprinkle on the rest of the cooking oil.

3. Put the roasting plate in the oven. Use a strong fire for 5 minutes and then turn down to a medium fire to cook 15-20 minutes. Take out and sprinkle on the Chinese prickly ash powder.

Features：Soft and succulent. Strongly aromatic.
Taste：Salty and delicious.

大葱烧豆腐

主料：豆腐 500 克

辅料：大葱 150 克、猪肉末 50 克

调料：酱油 30 克、料酒 5 克、味精 2 克、鸡汤 500 克、湿淀粉 15 克、油 100 克

制作：①将豆腐切成 3.5 厘米长、1.5 厘米宽、0.5 厘米厚的长方块，投入沸水锅中烫一下捞起，沥干水分；大葱洗干净，切成 4 厘米长粗丝。

②炒锅置火上，放油烧至七成热，下葱丝、肉末炒散，烹料酒，放入豆腐、酱油、鸡汤、味精用大火烧开，转小火烧 5 分钟，再转大火收干汤汁，用湿淀粉勾芡出锅。

特点：大葱浓香，豆腐热烫，汁浓味厚

口味：软嫩鲜香

Bean Curd with Scallions and Minced Meat

Ingredients:

500 grams (1.1 lb) bean curd
150 grams (0.33 lb) scallions
50 grams (0.11 lb) minced pork or other meat
30 grams (1 2/3 tbsp) soy sauce
5 grams (1 tsp) cooking wine
2 grams (1/3 tsp) salt
500 grams (1 cup) chicken soup
15 grams (1 3/4 tsp) mixture of cornstarch and water
100 grams (7 tbsp) cooking oil

Directions:

1. Cut the bean curd into slices 3.5 cm (1.4 inches) long, 1.5 cm (0.6 inch) wide and 0.5 cm (0.2 inch) thick. Quick-boil them and take out to drain off the water. Wash the scallions clean and cut into thick shreds 4 cm (1.6 inches) long.

2. Heat the oil in a wok to 180-200℃ (355-390˚F). Add the scallions and minced meat to stir-fry for 1 minute. Add the cooking wine, bean curd, soy sauce, chicken soup and MSG. Use a strong fire to bring to a boil and then turn to a low fire to simmer for 5 minutes. Turn to strong fire again to reduce the sauce. Thicken it with the mixture of cornstarch and water. The dish is now ready.

Features: Strongly aromatic with the scallions. The bean curd is richly flavored and the soup is very warm.

Taste: Tender and delicious.

大葱烧豆腐
Bean Curd with Scallions and Minced Meat

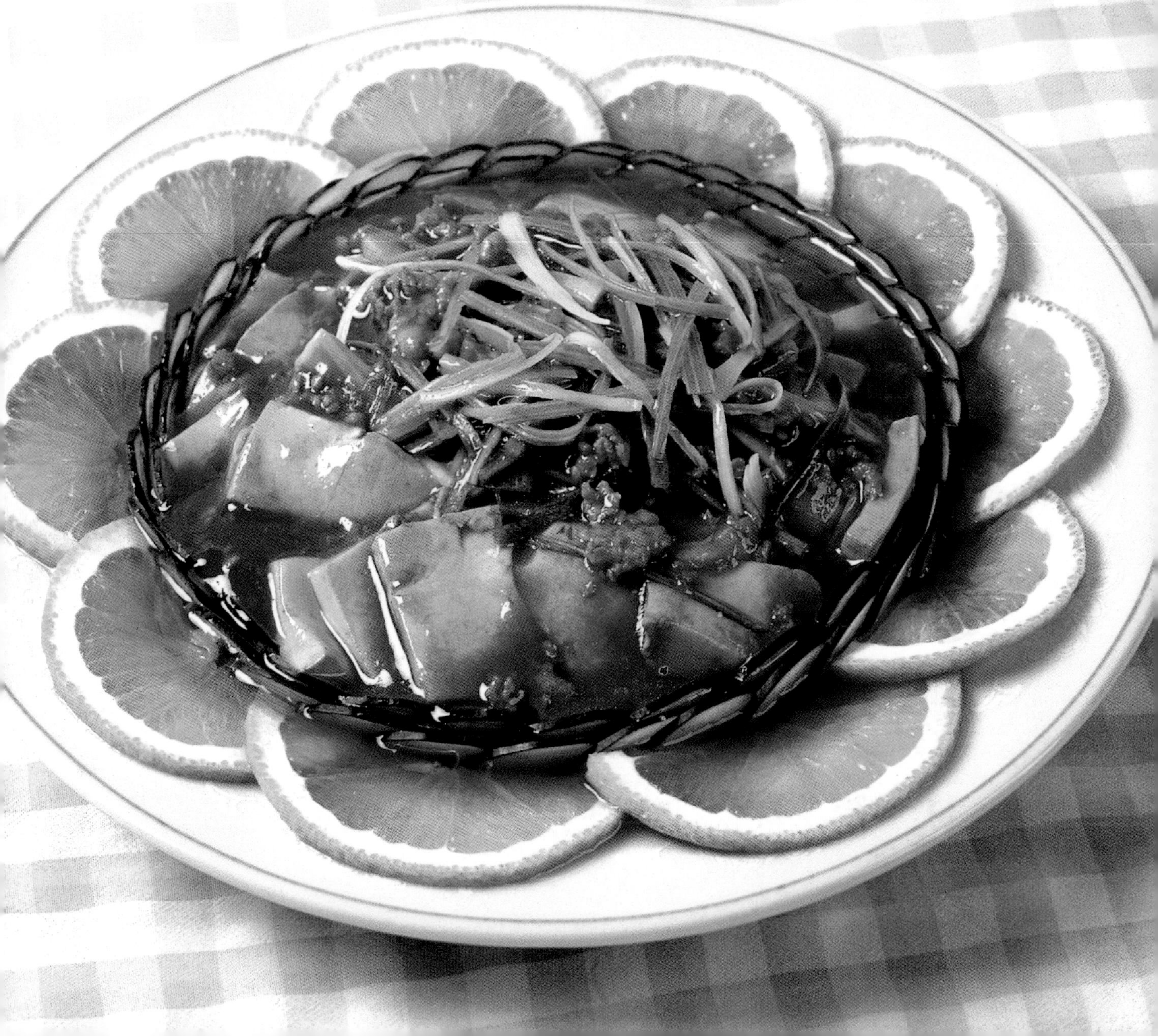

蜂窝豆腐

主料：冻豆腐 600 克（豆腐放冰柜低温冷冻，解冻后豆腐组织呈蜂窝状）

辅料：青椒 25 克、海米 25 克、火腿 50 克、虾籽 1 克

调料：盐 2 克、味精 1 克、鸡汤 350 克、湿淀粉 10 克、油 45 克

制作：①将冻豆腐切成长 5 厘米、宽 2 厘米的块，海米用水泡软洗净，青椒去蒂、籽洗净切成片，火腿洗净切片、用水煮熟备用。

②炒锅内放入鸡汤、冻豆腐、海米、青椒片、火腿片，大火煮沸，再加油、虾籽、盐、味精煮沸转小火焖烧 15 分钟，收干汤汁，用湿淀粉勾芡即可。

特点：鲜香可口，豆腐入味

口味：咸鲜

Honeycomb Bean Curd

Ingredients：
600 grams (1.2 lb) frozen bean curd (made by putting fresh bean curd in freezer and later, when defrosted, to find what looks like honeycombs on the surface of the bean curd)
25 grams (5/6 oz) green pepper
25 grams (5/6 oz) dried shrimp
50 grams (0.11 lb) ham
2 grams (1/3 tsp) salt
1 gram (1/4 tsp) MSG
350 grams (3/5-4/5 cup) chicken soup
10 grams (1 1/2 tsp) mixture of cornstarch and water
45 grams (3 1/3 tbsp) cooking oil

Directions：
1. Cut the defrosted bean curd into chunks 5 cm (2 inches) long and 2 cm (0.8 inch) wide. Soak the dried shrimps in water to soften them. Remove the stem and seeds of green pepper. Cut the ham into slices and boil them in water. Take out for later use.

2. Put the chicken soup in a wok along with the bean curd, shrimps, green pepper slices and ham slices. Use a strong fire to bring to a boil and add the cooking oil, salt and MSG. Turn to a low fire to cook for 15 minutes. Use a strong fire again to reduce some of the sauce and then thicken the dish with the mixture of cornstarch and water.

Features：Fragrant, and the bean curd has fully absorbed the sauce.
Taste：Salty and delicious.

蜂窝豆腐
Honeycomb Bean Curd

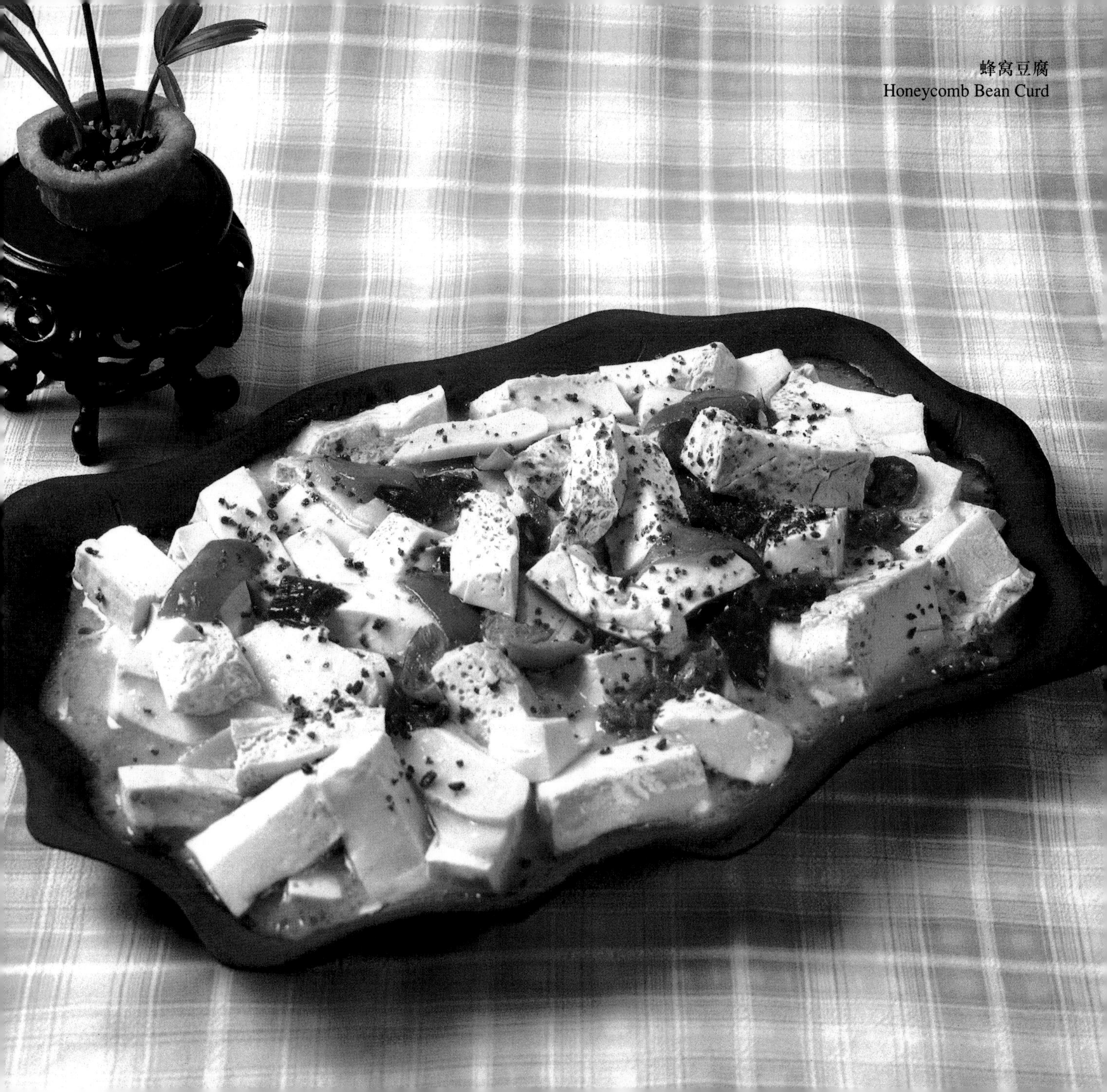

牛肉豆腐

主料：豆腐 300 克

辅料：牛里脊肉 300 克

调料：青蒜末 50 克、葱姜末各 10 克、酱油 30 克、糖 20 克、料酒 15 克、味精 2 克、鸡汤 750 克、五香粉 0.5 克、油 100 克、盐 1 克、鸡蛋清 1 只、干淀粉 10 克

制作：①牛里脊肉切成 5 厘米长、2 厘米宽的片，加鸡蛋清上浆；豆腐切成 5 厘米长、2 厘米宽、0.7 厘米厚的块，入沸锅焯水，捞出沥干水分。

②炒锅烧热，下油大火烧至高温放葱、姜和牛肉滑炒至出香味，下料酒、酱油、糖、五香粉翻炒，再加入鸡汤、豆腐大火烧沸转小火烧 10 分钟，收干汤汁，加味精调和口味，撒上青蒜末即可。

特点：滑嫩光亮

口味：味浓鲜香

Bean Curd with Beef

Ingredients：
300 grams (0.66 lb) bean curd
300 grams (0.66 lb) beef tenderloin
50 grams (0.11 lb) finely cut leeks
10 grams (1/3 oz) finely cut scallions
10 grams (1/3 oz) chopped ginger
30 grams (1 2/3 tbsp) soy sauce
20 grams (1 1/2 tbsp) sugar
15 gams (1 tbsp) cooking wine
2 grams (1/2 tsp) MSG
750 grams (1 1/2 cup) chicken soup
1/2 gram (1/10 tsp) five-flavored powder
100 grams (7 tbsp) cooking oil
1 gram (1/6 tsp) salt
1 egg white
10 grams (2 tsp) dry cornstarch

Directions：

1. Cut the beef tenderloin into slices 5 cm (2 inches) long and 2 cm (0.8 inch) wide. Mix the beef slices with the egg white and dry cornstarch. Cut the bean curd into slices of the same length and width, but much thicker (about 0.7 cm or 0.28 inch). Quick-boil the bean curd in water and take out to drain off the water.

2. Heat the oil to 200-220℃ (390-430°F) and stir-fry the beef slices, ginger and scallions for 1-2 minutes. Add the cooking wine, soy sauce, sugar and five-flavored powder, and turn several times. Put in the chicken soup and bean curd. Use a strong fire to bring to a boil and then turn to a low fire to cook for 10 minutes. Again use a strong fire to boil off some of the soup. Add the MSG and sprinkle on the finely cut leeks. The dish is now ready to serve.

Features：The dish is slippery and shinny.
Taste：Richly flavored and very delicious.

牛肉豆腐
Bean Curd with Beef

黄豆芽炖豆腐

主料：豆腐 200 克

辅料：黄豆芽 200 克，猪里脊肉 50 克

调料：葱姜末各 5 克、味精 1 克、盐 3 克、鸡汤 500 克、油 50 克

制作：①将豆腐切成 1.5 厘米见方、1 厘米厚的块，下沸锅焯水，捞出沥去水分；黄豆芽摘去须根洗净，入沸水略烫；猪肉切成细丝。

②炒锅烧热，下油烧至五成热，下葱姜末爆出香味，下猪肉丝滑炒至熟，倒入鸡汤，烧沸后，投入豆芽、豆腐烧 15 分钟至汤汁醇浓，黄豆芽酥烂，下盐和味精调好味出锅即可。

特点：汤汁乳白

口味：咸鲜

Stewed Bean Curd with Soy Bean Sprouts

Ingredients:
200 grams (0.44 lb) bean curd
200 grams (0.44 lb) soy bean sprouts
50 grams (0.11 lb) pork tenderloin
5 grams (1/6 oz) finely cut scallions
1 gram (1/4 tsp) MSG
3 grams (1/2 tsp) salt
500 grams (1 cup) chicken soup
50 grams (3 1/2 tbsp) cooking oil

Directions:
1. Reduce the bean curd to chunks 1.5 cm (0.6 inch) long and wide and 1 cm (0.4 inch) thick. Quick-boil in water and take out to drain off the water. Wash the soy bean sprouts clean and also quickly boil in water. Take out for later use. Cut the pork into thin shreds.

2. Heat the oil to 110-135℃ (230-275°F) and stir-fry the scallions until they produce a distinctive aroma. Add the pork shreds and stir-fry until they are done. Put in the chicken soup and bring to a boil. Add the soy bean sprouts and bean curd to cook for 15 minutes until the soup becomes thick and the bean sprouts are soft. Add the salt and MSG and take out to serve.

Features: The soup is milky white and looks really inviting.
Taste: Salty and delicious.

黄豆芽炖豆腐
Stewed Bean Curd with Soy Bean Sprouts

肉末豆腐羹

主料：豆腐 400 克

辅料：猪腿肉 50 克、木耳 25 克、小葱 10 克

调料：鸡汤 250 克、酱油 10 克、盐 2 克、味精 2 克、湿淀粉 10 克、油 75 克、料酒 5 克

制作：①将豆腐切成 1 厘米见方的丁，用沸水烫一下，再用冷水漂清。猪腿肉切成末，木耳用温水泡软洗净、切成丝，小葱洗净切细。

②炒锅烧热，放油 50 克烧至五成热倒入猪肉末煸炒至熟，烹料酒，倒入鸡汤，放入豆腐、木耳，再下酱油、盐煮沸转小火焖烧 10 分钟，待豆腐中间起蜂孔浮在汤面上，放入味精，用湿淀粉勾芡，倒入剩下的油，撒葱末，即出锅。

特点：汤稠似羹，入口爽滑

口味：豆腐鲜嫩可口

Bean Curd Soup with Minced Meat

Ingredients:
400 grams (0.88 lb) bean curd
50 grams (0.11 lb) pork leg meat
25 grams (5/6 oz) black fungus
10 grams (1/3 oz) tender scallions
250 grams (1/2 cup) chicken soup
10 grams (1 1/2 tsp) soy sauce
2 grams (1/3 tsp) salt
2 grams (1/2 tsp) MSG
10 grams (1 1/2 tsp) mixture of cornstarch and water
75 grams (5 1/2 tbsp) cooking oil
5 grams (1 tsp) cooking wine

Directions:
1. Cut the bean curd into cubes 1 cm (0.4 inch) long on each side. Boil in water and wash clean in cold water. Grind the pork leg into minced meat. Soak the black fungus in lukewarm water, wash clean and cut into shreds. Finely cut the scallions.

2. Heat 50 g (3 1/2 tbsp) oil to 110-135℃ (230-275˚F) and stir-fry the pork until it is done. Add the cooking wine, chicken soup, bean curd, fungus, soy sauce and salt. Use a strong fire to bring to a boil and turn to a low fire to cook for 10 minutes. When the bean curd comes to the top and floats in the soup, add the MSG and thicken the soup with the mixture of cornstarch and water. Sprinkle on the remaining oil and scallions. The dish is now ready to serve.

Features: The soup is slippery and succulent.
Taste: The bean curd is refreshing and delicious.

肉末豆腐羹
Bean Curd Soup with Minced Meat

翠绿腐竹

主料：腐竹 300 克

辅料：青椒 50 克

调料：糖 10 克、盐 3 克、麻油 15 克、味精 2 克、油 75 克、湿淀粉 10 克、鸡汤 50 克

制作：①腐竹用温水泡软洗净，切成长为 1.5 厘米的段；青椒去蒂、籽洗净，切成片。

②炒锅烧热，倒入油，烧至五成熟，投入腐竹、青椒煸炒，然后再下糖、盐、味精和鸡汤大火烧沸，用湿淀粉勾芡，淋上麻油即可。

特点：腐竹色白，青椒翠绿

口味：香鲜适口

Dried Bean Milk Cream with Green Pepper

Ingredients：

400 grams (0.88 lb) dried bean milk cream folded in long sections

50 grams (0.11 lb) green pepper

10 grams (2 tsp) sugar

3 grams (1/2 tsp) salt

15 grams (1 tbsp) sesame oil

2 grams (1/2 tsp) MSG

75 grams (5 1/2 tbsp) cooking oil

10 grams (1 1/2 tsp) mixture of cornstarch and water

50 grams (3 tbsp) chicken soup

Directions：

1. Soak the dried bean milk cream in lukewarm water to soften it. Cut into sections 1.5 cm (0.6 inch) long. Remove the stems and seeds of the green peppers and cut into slices.

2. Heat the oil in a wok to 110-135℃ (230-275°F) and stir-fry the sectioned dried bean milk cream and green pepper slices for 1 minute. Add the sugar, salt, MSG and chicken soup. Use a strong fire to bring to a boil and thicken the soup with the mixture of cornstarch and water. Sprinkle on the sesame oil and take out to serve.

Features：Nicely combined with the colors of white from the dried bean milk cream and green from the tender peppers.

Taste：Delicious.

翠绿腐竹
Dried Bean Milk Cream with Green Pepper

奶油腐竹蘑菇

主料：腐竹 250 克

辅料：油菜 25 克、鲜蘑菇 100 克

调料：盐 2 克、味精 1 克、料酒 10 克、糖 5 克、鸡汤 100 克、湿淀粉 10 克、油 75 克、姜末 2 克、奶油 30 克

制作：①腐竹用温水泡软洗净切成 3.5 厘米长的段，蘑菇洗净改切成两片，油菜洗净。

②炒锅烧热，下油加温放入姜末煸出香味，再下腐竹、蘑菇，煸约 1 分钟，烹料酒添入鸡汤、盐、糖、味精、油菜烧沸后下奶油，再用湿淀粉勾芡即可。

特点：汤色乳白，腐竹软嫩

口味：奶油醇香，口感软糯

Dried Bean Milk Cream with Mushrooms

Ingredients：
250 grams (0.55 lb) dried bean milk cream, already folded in long sections
25 grams (5/6 oz) green vegetables
100 grams (0.22 lb) fresh mushrooms
2 grams (1/3 tsp) salt
1 gram (1/4 tsp) MSG
10 grams (2 tsp) cooking wine
5 grams (1 tsp) sugar
100 grams (6 tbsp) chicken soup
10 grams (1 1/2 tsp) mixture of cornstarch and water
75 grams (5 1/2 tbsp) cooking oil
2 grams (1/15 oz) chopped ginger
30 grams (1 2/3 tbsp) milk cream

Directions：

1. Soak the dried bean milk cream and cut into sections 3.5 cm (1.4 inches) long. Cut each of the mushrooms into two halves. Wash the green vegetable clean.

2. Heat the oil to 110-135℃ (230-275° F) and stir-fry the ginger until it produces a distinctive aroma. Add the dried bean milk cream sections and mushrooms and stir-fry for 1 minute. Put in the cooking wine, chicken soup, salt, sugar, MSG and green vegetable. Use a strong fire to bring to a boil and then add the milk cream. Thicken the dish with the mixture of cornstarch and water. Take out and serve.

Features：Beautiful white soup with nice looking dried bean milk cream sections and green vegetables.
Taste：Strongly creamy and soft to the bite.

奶油腐竹蘑菇
Dried Bean Milk Cream with Mushrooms

咖喱百叶结

主料：百叶 400 克

调料：咖喱 5 克、盐 2 克、味精 1 克、油 40 克、葱段 5 克、姜片 3 克、湿淀粉 25 克、鸡汤 200 克

制作：①百叶切成长 10 厘米、宽 5 厘米的片，并卷起打结，入沸水锅焯后，再用清水洗净备用。

②炒锅烧热，下油烧至高温，下葱段姜片煸出香味，倒入鸡汤，放百叶，用大火烧沸，转小火煨 30 分钟，然后下咖喱、盐、味精，再转大火收干汤汁，用湿淀粉勾芡，即可。

特点：色泽金黄

口味：咖喱味浓郁

Curried Bean Curd Leaves

Ingredients：

400 grams (0. 88 lb) bean curd leaves (bean curd already made in the shape of sheets of paper)
5 grams (1 tsp) curry
2 grams (1/3 tsp) salt
1 gram (1/4 tsp) MSG
40 grams (3 tbsp) cooking oil
5 grams (1/6 oz) sectioned scallions
3 grams (1/10 oz) sliced ginger
25 grams (1 1/2 tbsp) mixture of cornstarch and water
200 grams (2/5 cup) chicken soup

Directions：

1. Cut the bean curd leaves (sheets) into slices 10 cm (4 inches) long and 5 cm (2 inches) wide. Roll each sheet up and make a tie in the middle. Quick-boil in water and run through cold water to wash clean for later use.

2. Heat the oil in a wok to 135-170℃ (275-340°F) and stir-fry the ginger and scallions until they produce a distinctive aroma. Add the chicken soup and bean curd sheets, and use a strong fire to bring to a boil. Turn to a low fire and simmer for 30 minutes. Add the curry, salt and MSG, and turn to a strong fire to reduce the soup. Thicken the sauce with the mixture of cornstarch and water and the dish is ready to serve.

Features：The dish has a shiny, golden color.
Taste：It has a strong fragrance of the curry.

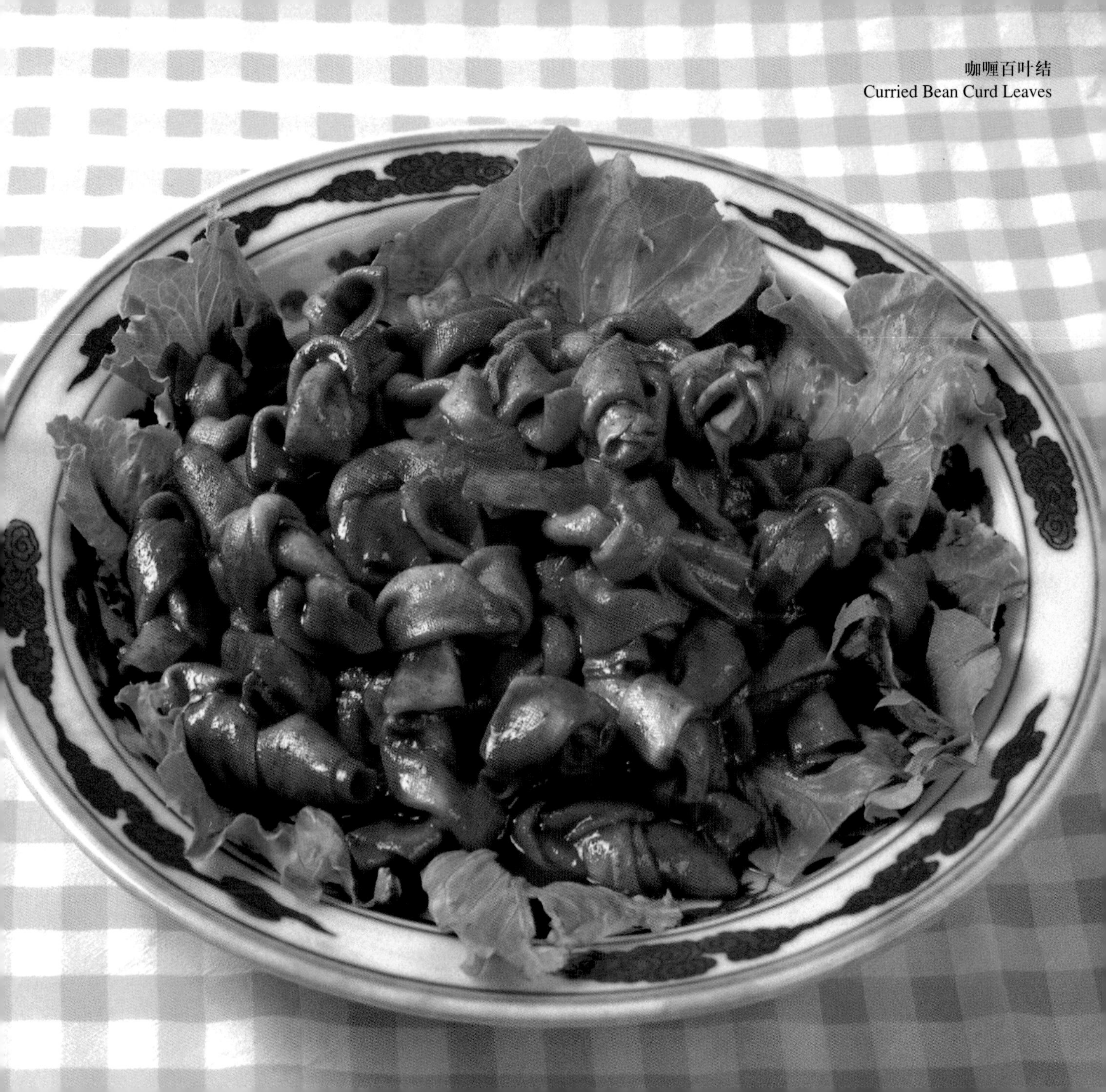

咖喱百叶结
Curried Bean Curd Leaves

五香酱干

主料：方豆腐干 500 克

调料：五香粉 10 克、甜豆酱 15 克、葱段 10 克、姜片 5 克、盐 5 克、味精 1 克、糖 10 克、油 500 克（实耗 100 克）、麻油 20 克、清水 250 克

制作：①将方干洗净，切成 4 厘米长、2 厘米宽的长方块。

②炒锅烧热，倒入油，烧至八成热，分次投入方干，炸至棕红色倒出沥油。

③锅中放麻油，烧热，下葱段、姜片、五香粉、甜面酱炒出香味，放入清水，大火煮沸约 10 分钟，倒入炸好的方干及盐、味精、糖用中火烧 15 分钟，使卤汁稠干出锅，捡去葱姜，待冷后即可食用。

特点：色泽酱红，质地酥软

口味：咸鲜带甜，五香味浓郁

Five-flavored Bean Curd Cheese

Ingredients:
500 grams (1.1 lb) bean curd cheese
10 grams (2 tsp) five-flavored powder
15 grams (1 3/4 tsp) sweet bean paste
10 grams (1/3 oz) sectioned scallions
5 grams (1/6 oz) ginger sliced
5 grams (5/6 tsp) salt
1 gram (1/4 tsp) MSG
10 grams (2 tsp) sugar
500 grams (1 cup) oil (only 1/5 to be consumed)
20 grams (1 1/2 tbsp) sesame oil
250 grams (1/2 cup) water

Directions:
1. Cut the bean curd cheese (usually made in the shape of squares) into rectangular chunks 4 cm (1.6 inches) long and 2 cm (0.8 inch) wide.

2. Heat the oil in the wok to 200-220℃ (390-430°F) and gradually put in the bean curd cheese. Deep-fry until they are brownish red. Take out and drain off the oil.

3. Put the sesame oil in a wok, heat it and stir-fry the scallions, ginger, five-flavored powder, and sweet bean paste until these produce a strong aroma. Add the water and use a strong fire to let it boil for 10 minutes. Put in the deep-fried bean curd cheese chunks, salt, MSG and sugar, and cook for 15 minutes over a medium fire. Take out when the soup becomes sticky. Pick out and get rid of the scallions and ginger. Let it cool off and then serve.

Features: Dark red in color, the bean curd cheese is very soft.
Taste: Salty with a sweet touch and a strong five-flavored taste.

五香酱干
Five-flavored Bean Curd Cheese

香炸豆沙包

主料：豆腐皮（12 厘米见方）24 张、青蚕豆 500 克

辅料：糖 300 克、糖桂花 15 克

调料：湿淀粉 15 克、色拉油 600 克

制作：①青蚕豆洗净、去皮，煮烂后压成豆沙备用。

②炒锅烧热，下油烧至四成热，放入豆沙煸炒至酥松后加糖，待糖溶化出锅晾凉即成豆沙馅。

③豆腐皮用凉水泡软，沥干水摊开放入豆沙馅，包成 4.6 厘米长、3.5 厘米宽的长方形，搭口处用湿淀粉封住，制成豆沙包生坯 24 只。

④炒锅烧热，倒入油，烧至八成热，分批下豆沙包生坯煎炸至金黄色时捞出沥油，装盘，抹上糖桂花即可。

特点：香酥爽口

口味：清香酥甜

Bean Dumplings

Ingredients:

24 sheets of bean curd peel, about 12 cm (4.8 inches) long each side

500 grams (1.1 lb) tender broad beans

300 grams (10 oz) sugar

15 grams (1/2 oz) mixture of sugar and sweetened osmanthus flower paste

15 grams (1 3/4 tsp) mixture of cornstarch and water

600 grams (1 1/5 cup) salad oil

Directions:

1. Wash the tender broad beans clean, remove the skin and boil them to make a paste.

2. Heat the oil in a wok to 70-100℃ (160-210˚F) and fry the bean paste until it is no longer sticky. Add the sugar and take out of the wok when the sugar melts. Let it cool off and the bean paste filling is made.

3. Soften the bean curd peels by soaking them in cold water. Drain off the water, spread them out and put the bean paste filling on each peel to produce 24 rectangular shaped dumplings 4.6 cm (1.8 inches) long and 3.5 cm (1.4 inches) wide. Seal them up in dumpling shape with some of the mixture of cornstarch and water.

4. Heat the oil in a wok to 200-220℃ (390-430˚F) and gradually deep-fry the dumplings until they are golden yellow in color. Drain off the oil and place on a plate. Sprinkle on the mixture of sugar and osmanthus flower paste.

Features: Crispy and refreshing.

Taste: Sweet and delicious.

香炸豆沙包
Bean Dumplings

三虾豆腐

主料：豆腐 400 克

辅料：虾仁 75 克、虾籽 5 克、虾脑 5 克

调料：料酒 5 克、味精 1 克、盐 2 克、鸡汤 250 克、油 25 克、湿淀粉 10 克

制作：①虾仁洗净用沸水烫熟；豆腐切成长 4 厘米、宽 2 厘米、厚 1 厘米的块，用沸水焯一下，并在冷水中漂凉。

②炒锅烧热，下油烧至四成热，下虾仁，烹料酒，下鸡汤、豆腐，大火烧开，撒入虾脑、虾籽，转小火烧 10 分钟后，下盐、味精，用湿淀粉勾芡起锅倒入汤碗中即可。

特点：色泽洁白

口味：鲜嫩可口

Bean Curd with Shrimps

Ingredients：
400 grams (0.88 lb) bean curd
75 grams (0.165 lb) shelled shrimps
5 grams (1 tsp) cooking wine
1 gram (1/4 tsp) MSG
2 grams (1/3 tsp) salt
250 grams (1/2 cup) chicken soup
25 grams (1 2/3 tbsp) cooking oil
10 grams (1 1/2 tsp) mixture of cornstarch and water

Directions：
1. Wash the shrimps clean and pour on boiling water to bring them to a half cooked state. Cut the bean curd into chunks 4 cm (1.6 inches) long, 2 cm (0.8 inch) wide and 1 cm (0.4 inch) thick. Quick-boil these chunks in water and run them through cold water to cool them off.

2. Heat the oil to 70-100℃ (160-210°F) and put in the ingredients in the order of shrimps, cooking wine, chicken soup and bean curd chunks. Use a strong fire to bring to a boil and then turn to a low fire to cook for 10 minutes. Add the salt and MSG and thicken with the mixture of cornstarch and water. Pour out into a soup bowl to serve.

Features：It looks inviting.
Taste：Refreshing and delicious.

三虾豆腐
Bean Curd with Shrimps

花生米拌香干

主料：花生仁 100 克、香豆腐干 250 克

调料：葱 5 克、干红辣椒 10 克、盐 3 克、味精 2 克、油 100 克（实耗 25 克）、麻油 5 克

制作：①炒锅烧热，下油烧至四成热，倒下花生仁小火炸熟，倒出沥油。

②香豆腐干切成 1.2 厘米见方的丁，在沸水中略煮烫倒出沥干水分。葱、红辣椒洗净切段。

③将花生仁、香豆腐干拌和在一起，加盐、味精调好味，淋上麻油、撒上葱、红辣椒（葱、红辣椒过热油更好）即可。

特点：香味浓郁

口味：花生松脆，香干鲜香

Bean Curd Cheese with Peanuts

Ingredients:

100 grams (0.22 lb) shelled peanuts
250 grams (0.55 lb) bean curd cheese (usually in square shapes)
5 grams (1/6 oz) scallions
10 grams (1/3 oz) dried red chilies
3 grams (1/2 tsp) salt
2 grams (1/2 tsp) MSG
100 grams (7tbsp) oil(only 25 g or 1 2/3 tbsp to be consumed)
5 grams (1 tsp) sesame oil

Directions:

1. Heat the oil in a wok to 70-100℃ (160-210°F) and fry the peanuts over a low fire. Take them out and drain off the oil.

2. Cut the bean curd cheese into dices 1.2 cm (0.48 inch) long each side. Quick-boil them in water and take out to drain off the water. Cut the scallions and the red chilies into sections.

3. Mix the peanuts and bean curd cheese dices. Add the salt and MSG, and then sprinkle on the sesame oil, scallions and red chilies. Alternatively, stir-fry the scallions and red chilies before putting them together with the peanuts and bean curd and it will enrich the taste.

Features: Richly fragrant.
Taste: The peanuts are crispy and the bean curd cheese is especially delicious.

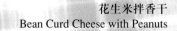

青豆炒香干

主料：香豆腐干 200 克

辅料：罐装青豆 50 克

调料：盐 3 克、味精 1 克、油 50 克

制作：①先将香干切成 0.8 厘米见方的丁，用沸水焯一下，待用。

②青豆用沸水（水中加盐 2 克）煮熟。

③炒锅烧热，下油烧至五成热，倒入青豆和香干略炒几下，下盐、味精调好口味出锅。

特点：黄绿相间

口味：鲜香

Stir-fried Bean Curd Cheese with Peas

Ingredients：

200 grams (0.44 lb) bean curd cheese
50 grams (0.11 lb) canned green peas
3 grams (1/2 tsp) salt
1 gram (1/4 tsp) MSG
50 grams (3 1/2 tbsp) cooking oil

Directions：

1. Cut the bean curd cheese into dices 0.8 cm (0.3 inch) long each side and quick-boil in water for later use.

2. Boil the peas until they are done. Add 2 g (1/3 tsp) of salt in the water when boiling the peas.

3. Heat the oil in a wok to 110-135℃ (230-275˚F). Add the green peas and bean curd cheese dices and stir-fry for 1 minute. Add the salt and MSG and take out to serve.

Features：Nice combination of green and yellow colors.
Taste：Very delicious.

青豆炒香干
Stir-fried Bean Curd Cheese with Peas

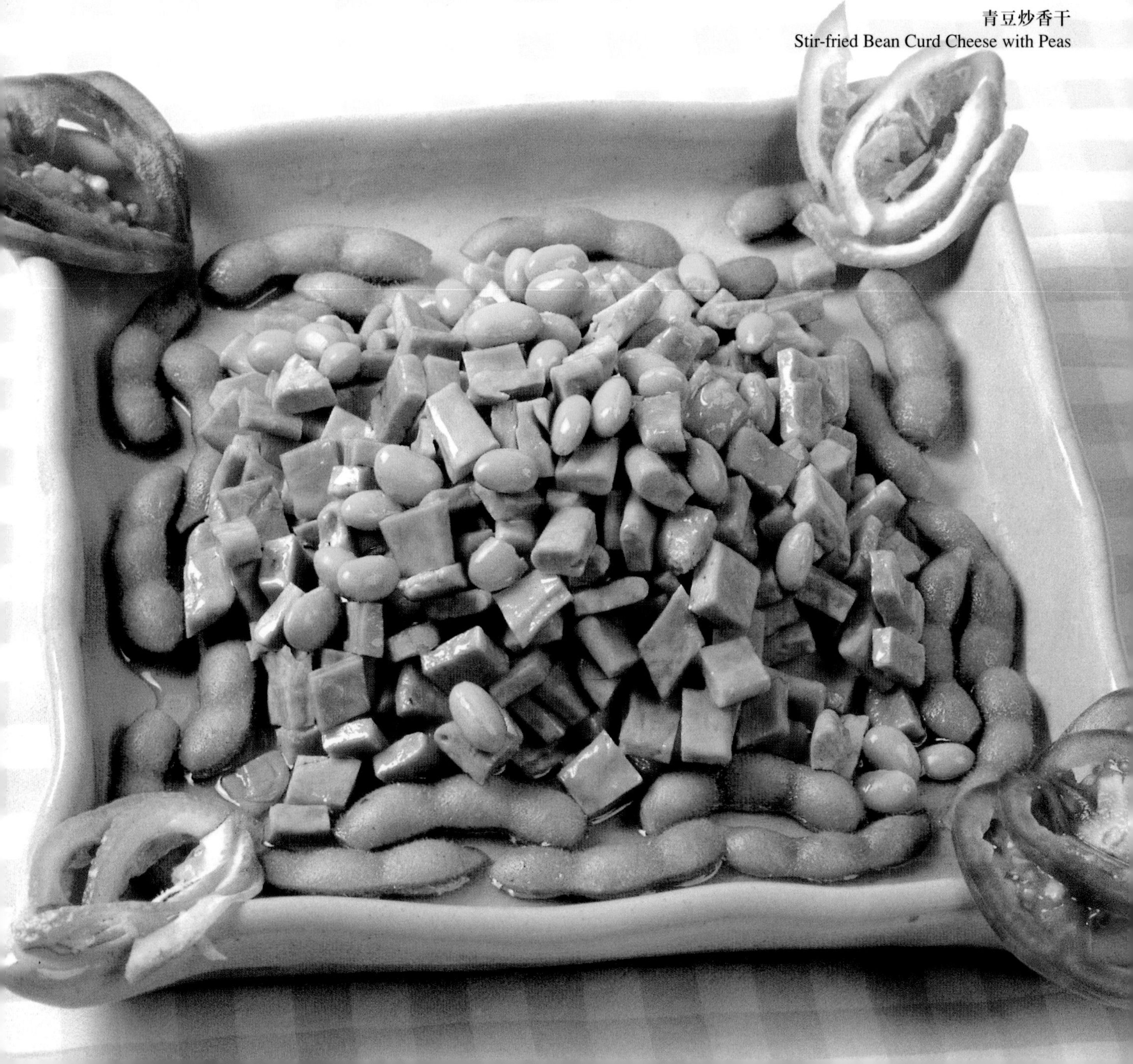

海米拌干丝

主料：白豆腐干 200 克

辅料：海米 25 克

调料：盐 2 克、味精 1 克、油 25 克、葱末 5 克

制作：①白豆腐干切 6 厘米长、0.3 厘米粗的细丝，用沸水焯一下，待用。

②海米用温水泡软洗净，上笼屉蒸半小时取出，待用。

③将海米拌入白干丝中，加盐、味精调好口味；另将炒锅烧热下油，烧至五成热，投入葱花，炒出香味熬成葱油，淋入海米白干丝内，拌匀即可。

特点：海鲜味浓

口味：咸鲜适口

Shredded Bean Curd Cheese with Dried Shrimps

Ingredients：
200 grams (0.44 lb) white bean curd cheese
25 grams (5/6 oz) dried shrimps
2 grams (1/3 tsp) salt
1 gram (1/4 tsp) MSG
25 grams (1 2/3 tbsp) cooking oil
5 grams (1/6 oz) scallions finely cut

Directions：

1. Cut the white bean curd cheese into fine shreds 6 cm (2.4 inches) long and 0.3 cm (0.12 inch) thick. Quick-boil in water and take out for later use.

2. Soak the dried shrimps in lukewarm water, steam for 30 minutes and take out for later use.

3. Mix the shrimps with the bean curd cheese shreds. Add the salt and MSG. Meanwhile heat the oil in a wok to 110-135℃ (230-275°F) and stir-fry the scallions until they produce a strong aroma. Sprinkle the oil on the shrimps and bean curd. Mix well and serve.

Features：The dish has a strong seafood flavor.
Taste：Salty to the right taste.

海米拌干丝
Shredded Bean Curd Cheese with Dried Shrimps

芹菜干丝

主料：白豆腐干 200 克

辅料：芹菜 150 克、胡萝卜 50 克

调料：盐 2 克、味精 1 克、油 20 克

制作：①白豆腐干切 6 厘米长、0.5 厘米粗的细丝，用沸水焯一下待用。

②芹菜洗净，去叶，胡萝卜洗净，都切成 5 厘米长、0.3 厘米粗的细丝，用沸水焯熟，待用。

③将芹菜丝、胡萝卜丝、白干丝一同放在碗中，加盐、味精调好味。

④另将炒锅内加入油，烧至高温，浇在芹菜丝、胡萝卜丝、干丝内拌匀即可。

特点：绿白交映，色泽淡雅

口味：咸鲜爽口

Shredded Bean Curd Cheese with Celery

Ingredients：

200 grams (0.44 lb) bean curd cheese
150 grams (0.33 lb) celery
50 grams (0.11 lb) carrots
2 grams (1/3 tsp) salt
1 gram (1/4 tsp) MSG
20 grams (1 1/2 tbsp) cooking oil

Directions：

1. Cut the bean curd cheese into shreds 6 cm (2.4 inches) long and 0.5 cm (0.2 inch) thick and quickly boil in water.

2. Get rid of the leaves of the celery and wash clean. Also wash the carrots. Cut both celery and carrots into shreds 5 cm (2 inches) long and 0.3 cm (0.12 inch) thick and quickly boil in water.

3. Put all the three kinds of shreds in a bowl. Add the salt and MSG and mix well.

4. Heat the oil in a wok to 180-200℃ (390-430°F) and sprinkle the oil on the mixture. Mix well and serve.

Features：Elegant looking with the combination of white, orange and green colors.
Taste：Refreshing and soothing to the bite.

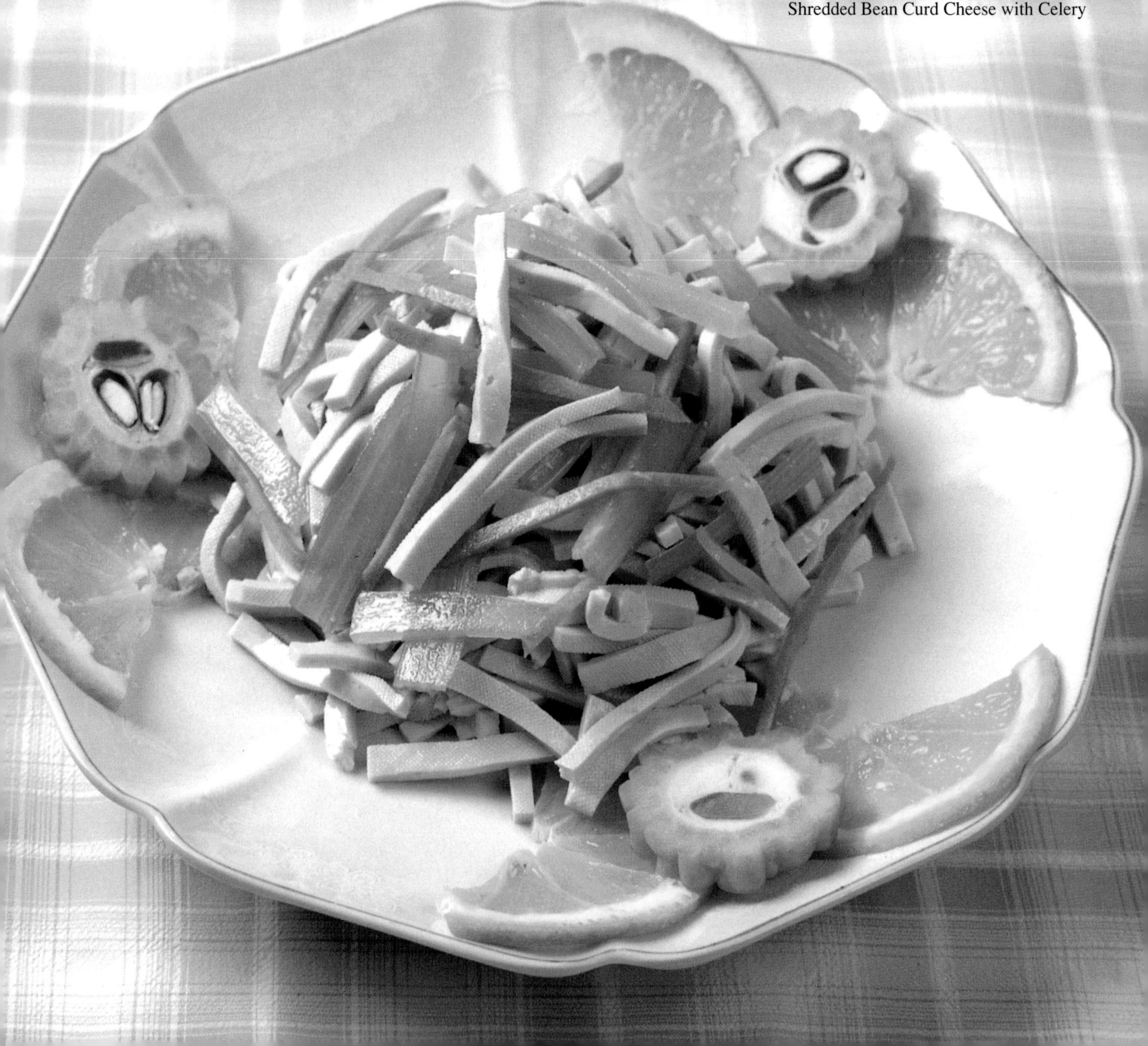

芹菜干丝
Shredded Bean Curd Cheese with Celery

三丝银芽

主料：绿豆芽 25 克

辅料：香菇 25 克、青椒 250 克、胡萝卜 50 克

调料：姜丝 5 克、盐 2 克、味精 1 克、麻油 5 克、花生油 20 克

制作：①绿豆芽掐去尾须，洗净，用沸水焯一下待用。

②香菇用温水泡软去蒂，切成丝；青椒去蒂、籽，洗净也切成丝；胡萝卜洗净，刨去表皮，切成 6 厘米长、0.3 厘米粗细的丝；姜去皮也切成细丝。

③炒锅烧热，下油烧至五成热爆香姜丝，投入香菇丝、青椒丝、胡萝卜丝煸炒，然后加盐、味精再煸炒至熟，投入绿豆芽，淋上麻油翻炒拌匀即可。

特点：色彩绚丽

口味：鲜脆爽口

Bean Sprouts with Vegetables

Ingredients：

25 grams (5/6 oz) green bean sprouts
25 grams (5/6 oz) dried mushrooms
250 grams (0.55 lb) green peppers
50 grams (0.11 lb) carrots
5 grams (1/6 oz) ginger cut into shreds
2 grams (1/3 tsp) salt
1 gram (1/4 tsp) MSG
5 grams (1 tsp) sesame oil
20 grams (1 1/2 tbsp) cooking oil

Directions：

1. Remove the roots of the bean sprouts and quick-boil in water.

2. Soak the dried mushrooms in lukewarm water to make them soft. Remove the end of the stems and cut into shreds. Remove the stems and seeds of the green peppers and cut into shreds. Remove the skin of the carrots and cut into shreds 6 cm (2.4 inches) long and 0.3 cm (0.12 inch) thick. Cut the ginger into fine shreds.

3. Heat the oil in a wok to 110-135℃ (230-275˚F) and quick-fry the ginger shreds. Add the shredded mushrooms, green peppers and carrots and stir-fry to mix well. Add the salt and MSG and continue to stir-fry until they are done. Add the bean sprouts, sprinkle on the sesame oil and take out to serve.

Features：Beautiful with colors.
Taste：Crispy and refreshingly delicious.

三丝银芽
Bean Sprouts with Vegetables

大煮干丝

主料：豆腐干 500 克

辅料：鸡脯肉 50 克、虾仁 50 克、火腿 50 克、油 100 克

调料：盐 3 克、味精 2 克、鸡汤 350 克、胡椒粉 5 克、料酒 10 克、姜 5 克、葱 5 克

制作：①将豆腐干切成 6 厘米长、0.3 厘米粗的细丝，用沸水煮 5 分钟，用冷水漂清。

②鸡脯肉、火腿分别用沸水煮熟与姜、葱一起切成同豆腐干丝一样粗的细丝，待用；虾仁用沸水烫熟。

③炒锅烧热，下油烧至五成热，下鸡丝、火腿丝略炒，烹料酒，下鸡汤、豆腐干丝，大火烧沸，下盐、味精、姜丝、葱丝转小火焖烧 10 分钟，撒上胡椒粉、虾仁出锅装盘。

特点：干丝绵软爽口，配料色彩鲜明

口味：汤汁醇厚味美

Bean Curd Cheese with Assorted Meats

Ingredients：

500 grams (1.1 lb) bean curd cheese
50 grams (0.11 lb) chicken breast
50 grams (0.11 lb) shelled shrimps
50 grams (0.11 lb) ham
100 grams (7 tbsp) cooking oil
3 grams (1/2 tsp) salt
2 grams (1/2 tsp) MSG
350 grams (3-4/5 cup) chicken soup
5 grams (1 tsp) pepper powder
10 grams (2 tsp) cooking wine
5 grams (1/6 oz) ginger
5 grams (1/6 oz) scallions

Directions：

1. Cut the bean curd cheese into shreds 6 cm (2.4 inches) long and 0.3 cm (0.12 inch) thick. Quick-boil in water and then wash with cold water.

2. Boil the chicken breast and ham separately until they are done. Cut them as well as the ginger and scallions into shreds of the same size as the bean curd cheese. Pour boiling water on the shrimps to cook them.

3. Heat the oil in a wok to 110-135℃ (230-275˚F) and stir-fry the chicken shreds and ham shreds. Add the cooking wine, chicken soup and bean curd cheese, and bring to a boil over a strong fire. Put in the salt, MSG, ginger and scallions and turn to a low fire to cook for 10 minutes. Sprinkle on the pepper powder and shrimps. Now the dish is ready to serve.

Features: The dish is beautifully colored and the shredded ingredients are soft to the bite.

Taste: Richly flavored.

大煮干丝
Bean Curd Cheese with Assorted Meats

青椒银芽

主料：绿豆芽 200 克

辅料：青椒 100 克

调料：油 10 克、盐 2 克、味精 1 克

制作：①将青椒洗净，去蒂、籽切成 6 厘米长、0.3 厘米粗的细丝。

②绿豆芽去须洗净，沥干水分。

③将绿豆芽、青椒一起倒入沸水中烫煮 1 分钟，捞出沥干水分装盘。盘中放入油、盐、味精拌均匀即可。

特点：绿白相间，清新淡雅

口味：脆嫩清爽，咸鲜可口

Bean Sprouts with Green Pepper

Ingredients：

200 grams (0.44 lb) green bean sprouts
100 grams (0.22 lb) green pepper
10 grams (2 tsp) cooking oil
2 grams (1/3 tsp) salt
1 gram (1/4 tsp) MSG

Directions：

1. Remove the stems and seeds of the green peppers and cut into shreds 6 cm (2.4 inches) long and 0.3 cm (0.12 inch) thick.

2. Remove the roots of the bean sprouts. Wash them clean and drain off the water.

3. Boil the bean sprouts and shredded green pepper in water for 1 minute. Take out, drain off the water and place on a plate. Add oil, salt and MSG and mix well before serving.

Features：The elegant looking dish with the combination of green and white colors is characterized by its refreshing taste.

Taste: Crispy, salty and delicious.

青椒银芽
Bean Sprouts with Green Pepper

茄汁干丝

主料：白豆腐干 200 克

辅料：洋葱 50 克

调料：番茄酱 30 克、油 40 克、盐 2 克、味精 1 克、糖 15 克

制作：①白豆腐干切成 6 厘米长、0.5 厘米粗的丝，用沸水烫一下用冷水漂清。洋葱洗净，切丝。

②炒锅烧热，下油烧至五成热，下番茄酱，边炒边投入盐、糖、味精，然后倒入白干丝、洋葱丝，中火烧至汤汁稠干，出锅装盘。

特点：色泽红润

口味：茄汁味浓

Bean Curd Cheese with Tomato Sauce

Ingredients：

200 grams (0.44 lb) bean curd cheese
50 grams (0.11 lb) onions
30 grams (1 2/3 tbsp) tomato sauce
40 grams (3 tbsp) cooking oil
2 grams (1/3 tsp) salt
1 gram (1/4 tsp) MSG
15 grams (1 tbsp) sugar

Directions：

1. Cut the bean curd cheese into shreds 6 cm (2.4 inches) long and 0.5 cm (0.2 inch) thick. Quick-boil in water and then run through cold water to wash clean. Cut the onions into shreds of similar size.

2. Heat the oil in a wok to 110-135℃ (230-275˚F). Add the tomato sauce and stir while adding the salt, sugar and MSG. Then put in the shredded bean curd cheese and onions and use medium fire to cook until the soup thickens and becomes sticky. Take out and serve.

Features：Reddish in color.
Taste：With a strong nice taste of tomatoes.

茄汁干丝
Bean Curd Cheese with Tomato Sauce

火腿末拌豆腐

主料：豆腐 400 克

辅料：火腿 50 克、甜面酱 40 克

调料：油 20 克、姜末 10 克、葱末 10 克、盐 2 克、味精 1 克、麻油 15 克

制作：①火腿用水煮熟，切成末。小火加油放入甜面酱熬熟。

②将豆腐切成 2 厘米见方的块，放在漏勺中，用沸水烫透，倒出沥干水分，装盘。

③将盐、味精、姜末、葱末、火腿末、甜面酱，撒在豆腐上，淋上麻油，上席由食者自己拌用。

特点：红黄黑三色相间，色彩诱人

口味：咸鲜嫩滑

Bean Curd with Ham

Ingredients:

400 gams (0.88 lb) bean curd
50 grams (0.11 lb) ham
40 grams (2 1/4 tbsp) sweet bean paste
20 grams (1 1/2 tbsp) cooking oil
10 grams (1/3 oz) chopped ginger
10 grams (1/3 oz) finely cut scallions
2 grams (1/3 tsp) salt
1 gram (1/4 tsp) MSG
15 grams (1 tbsp) sesame oil

Directions:

1. Boil the ham until it is done and cut into fine cubes. Put the oil in a wok and cook the sweet bean paste over a low fire.

2. Cut the bean curd into dices 2 cm (0.8 inch) long on each side. Place them in a strainer and run boiling water through the bean curd. Drain off the water and put on a plate.

3. Sprinkle the salt, MSG, ginger, scallions, ham and sweet bean paste on the bean curd. Also sprinkle on the sesame oil. Mix before serving.

Features: The combination of red, yellow and black colors makes the dish very enticing.

Taste: Salty and slippery.

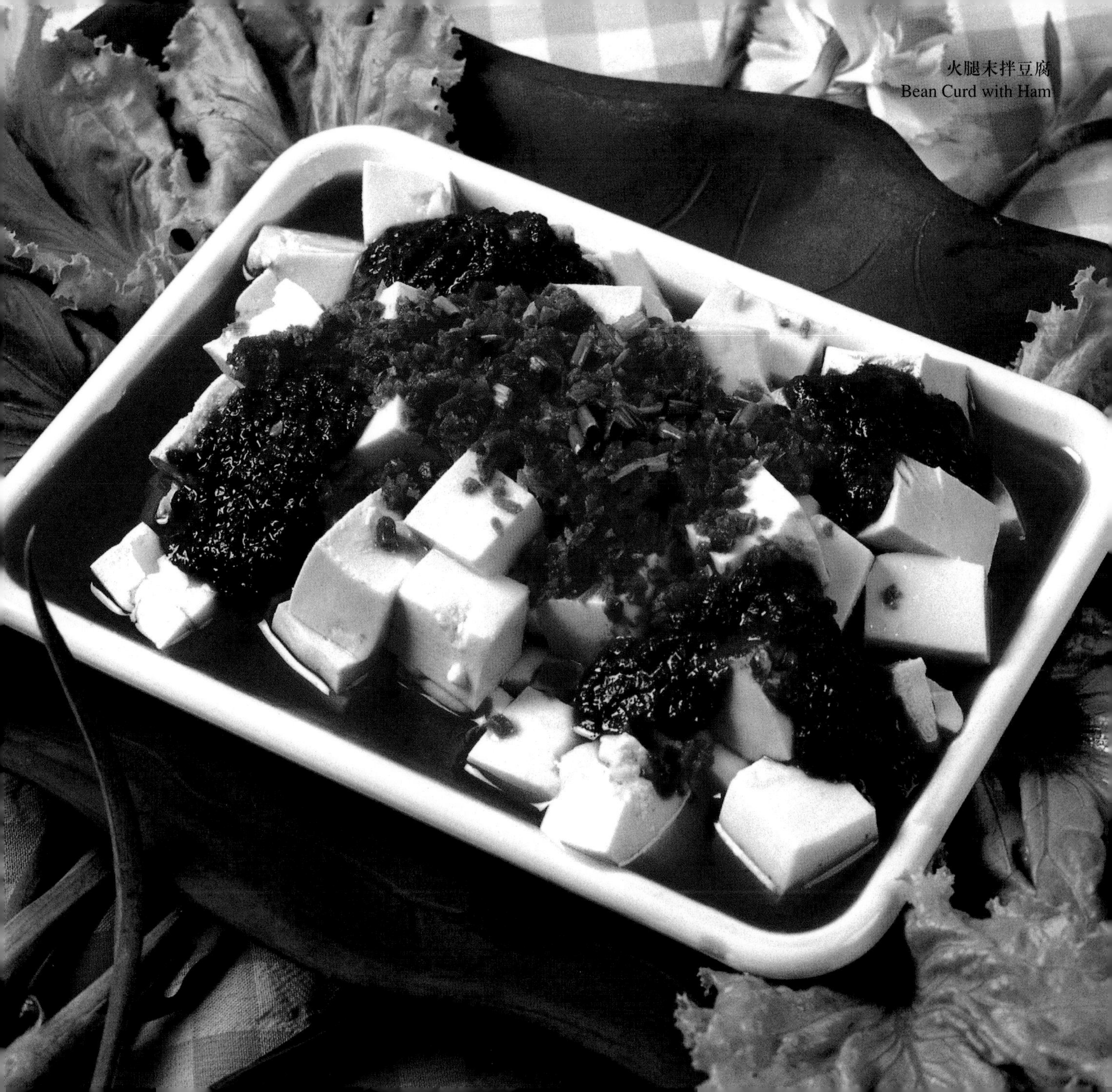

火腿末拌豆腐
Bean Curd with Ham

素拌黄豆芽

主料：黄豆芽 200 克

辅料：胡萝卜 5 克、小青菜或青椒 25 克

调料：盐 2 克、味精 1 克、熟油 5 克

制作：①将黄豆芽去须、洗净，胡萝卜、小青菜或青椒洗净；均切成 5 厘米长、3 厘米宽的片。

②将黄豆芽、胡萝卜片、小青菜在沸水中烫熟，调入盐、味精、油，充分拌匀装盘。

特点：色彩绚丽，营养丰富

口味：咸鲜

Soy Bean Sprouts with Sliced Carrot & Green Pepper

Ingredients：
200 grams (0.44 lb) soy bean sprouts
5 grams (1/6 oz) carrot
25 grams (5/6 oz) green vegetable or green pepper
2 grams (1/3 tsp) salt
1 gram (1/4 tsp) MSG
5 grams (1 tsp) cooked cooking oil

Directions：
1. Remove the roots of the soy bean sprouts and wash clean. Wash the carrot and green vegetable (or green pepper) and cut into thin slices (or sections in the case of green vegetables) 5 cm (2 inches) long and 3 cm (1.2 inches) wide.

2. Boil the soy bean sprouts, sliced carrot and green vegetable (pepper). Take out. Add salt, MSG and oil, and mix well. Put on a serving plate.

Features：The dish is beautifully colored and very nourishing.
Taste：Salty and delicious.

素拌黄豆芽
Soy Bean Sprouts with Sliced Carrot & Green Pepper

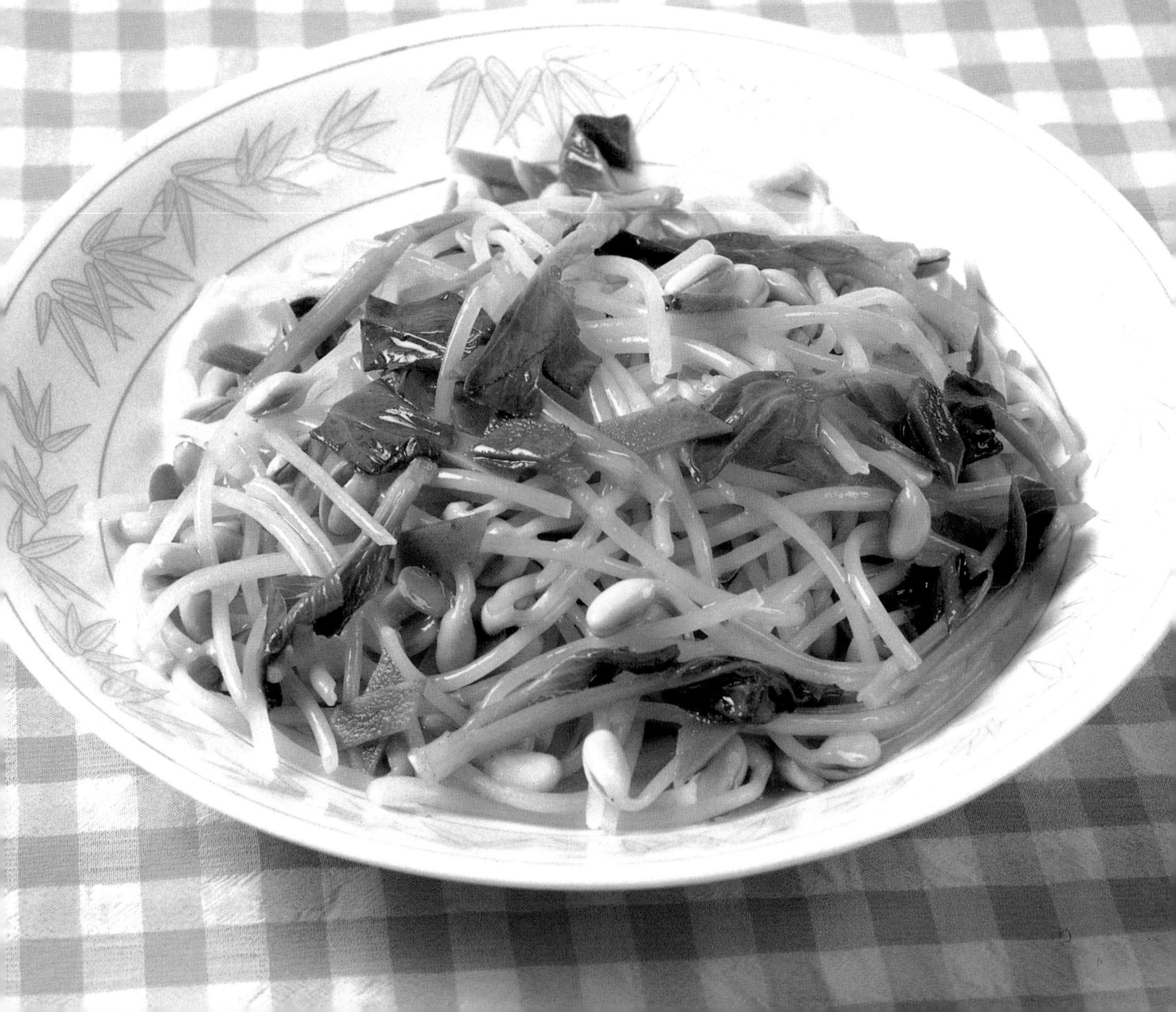

咸蛋炖豆腐

主料：豆腐 250 克

辅料：咸鸭蛋 2 只

调料：盐 2 克、味精 1 克、葱末 5 克、油 10 克、料酒 5克

制作：①将豆腐切 3 厘米长、2 厘米宽、1 厘米厚的块装入盘周围。咸鸭蛋打碎，将蛋黄放在豆腐中间，撒上盐、味精、料酒，上笼屉蒸 15 分钟取出。

②炒锅烧热，下油烧至高温，投入葱末，炒出香味，淋在咸蛋炖豆腐上即可。

特点：营养丰富

口味：豆腐滑嫩，口味咸鲜

Bean Curd Stewed with Salted Duck Eggs

Ingredients：
250 grams (0.55 lb) bean curd
2 salted duck eggs
2 grams (1/3 tsp) salt
1 gram (1/4 tsp) MSG
5 grams (1/6 oz) finely cut scallions
10 grams (2 tsp) cooking oil
5 grams (1 tsp) cooking wine

Directions：
1. Cut the bean curd into chunks 3 cm (1.2 inches) long, 2 cm (0.8 inch) wide and 1 cm (0.4 inch) thick. Place them in a circle on the edge of a serving plate. Beat the salted duck eggs and put in the center of the bean curd. Sprinkle on the salt, MSG and cooking wine and steam for 15 minutes.

2. Heat the oil to 180-200℃ (355-390°F) and stir-fry the scallions until there is a distinctive aroma. Sprinkle the oil and scallions on the bean curd and duck eggs.

Features：Highly nourishing.
Taste：The bean curd is slippery and tender and the dish is salty and delicious.

咸蛋炖豆腐
Bean Curd Stewed with Salted Duck Eggs

鸡蛋蒸豆腐

主料：豆腐 100 克

辅料：鸡蛋 3 只

调料：盐 2 克、味精 1 克、鸡汤 200 克、麻油 5 克、葱末 5 克、料酒 5 克

制作：先将鸡蛋打碎，蛋液打散放在碗中，再将豆腐搅碎一同放在蛋液中，注入鸡汤、盐、味精，上笼蒸 15 分钟，待蛋液凝结取出，撒上葱花，淋上麻油。

特点：色泽奶黄

口味：咸鲜滑嫩

Steamed Bean Curd and Eggs

Ingredients：
100 grams (0.22 lb) bean curd
3 chicken eggs
2 grams (1/3 tsp) salt
1 gram (1/4 tsp) MSG
200 grams (2/5 cup) chicken soup
5 grams (1 tsp) sesame oil
5 grams (1/6 oz) finely cut scallions
5 grams (1 tsp) cooking wine

Directions：
Whip the eggs in a bowl, crush the bean curd and place in the bowl with the eggs. Add the chicken soup, salt and MSG, and steam for 15 minutes. When the eggs have solidified, take out and sprinkle on the scallions and sesame. It is now ready to serve.

Features：With a slightly yellowish milky color.
Taste：Salty, slippery and delicious.

鸡蛋蒸豆腐
Steamed Bean Curd and Eggs

文丝豆腐

主料：豆腐 150 克

辅料：香菇 15 克、胡萝卜 15 克、葱 10 克

调料：盐 3 克、鸡汤 250 克、味精 2 克、湿淀粉 50 克、油 50 克、料酒 10 克

制作：①豆腐切 0.2 厘米粗的细丝，用沸水烫一下待用。
②香菇用温水泡软去蒂洗净切成细丝，胡萝卜切 6 厘米长、0.2 厘米粗的细丝，葱也切成 6 厘米长的丝。
③炒锅烧热，下油烧至五成热，投入葱丝、香菇丝、胡萝卜丝略炒，烹入料酒，注入鸡汤，大火烧沸，转小火，下豆腐丝、盐、味精，用湿淀粉勾芡即出锅。

特点：色彩绚丽

口味：咸鲜

Stewed Shredded Bean Curd

Ingredients：

150 grams (0.33 lb) bean curd
15 grams (1/2 oz) dried mushrooms
15 grams (1/2 oz) carrots
10 grams (1/3 oz) finely cut scallions
3 grams (1/2 tsp) salt
2 grams (1/2 tsp) MSG
250 grams (1/2 cup) chicken soup
50 grams (2 2/3 tbsp) mixture of cornstarch and water
50 grams (3 1/2 tbsp) cooking oil
10 grams (2 tsp) cooking wine

Directions：

1. Cut the bean curd into fine shreds 0.2 cm (0.08 inch) thick and quick-boil in water.

2. Soak the dried mushrooms in lukewarm water to soften them. Remove the end of the stems, wash clean and cut into fine shreds. Cut the carrots into shreds 6 cm (2.4 inches) long and 0.2 cm (0.08 inch) thick. Also cut the scallions into shreds of the same length.

3. Heat the oil in a wok to 110-135℃ (230-275°F). Add the scallions, mushrooms and carrots, and quick-stir-fry. Then add the cooking wine and chicken soup and bring to a boil over a strong fire.

Features：Nicely colored
Taste：Salty and delicious.

文丝豆腐
Stewed Shredded Bean Curd

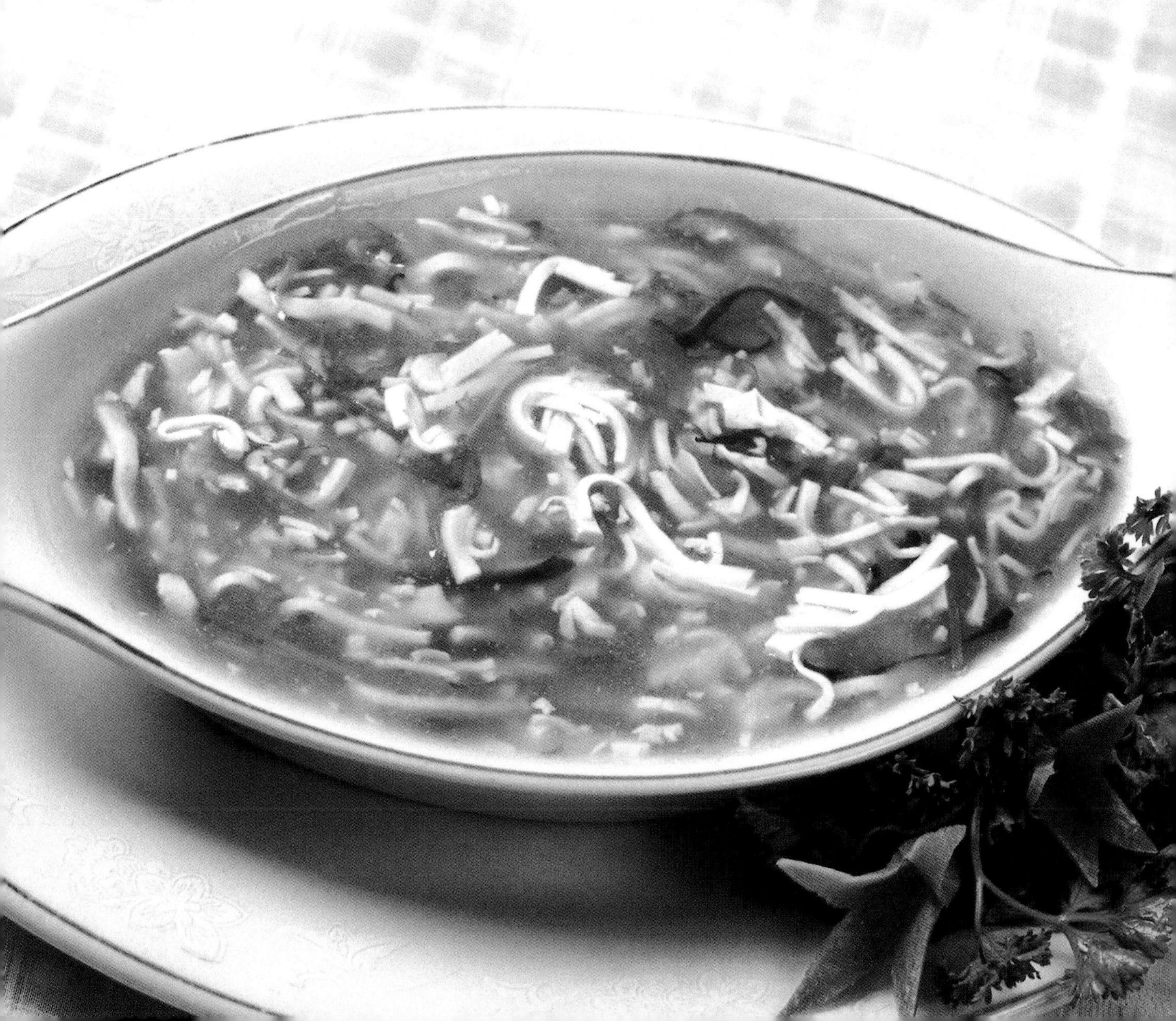

豆腐饺

主料：豆腐 400 克

辅料：虾仁 100 克、猪肉 100 克、生菜 20 克

调料：盐 3 克、味精 1.5 克、水 500 克

制作：①豆腐去老皮，拌成茸。

②虾仁和猪肉分别斩切成茸，各放入盐 1 克和味精 0.5 克，搅拌上劲待用。

③取豆腐茸 40 克平摊在纱布上，再包入虾茸、猪肉茸 20 克，连同纱布放在笼上蒸熟，即成豆腐饺（依照此法共做 8—10 个）。

④将豆腐饺放入烧沸的水中，加盐 1 克、味精 0.5 克调好味倒入碗中，各式蔬菜装点即可。

特点：形如饺子

口味：鲜嫩

Bean Curd Dumplings

Ingredients：
400 grams (0.88 lb) bean curd
100 grams (0.22 lb) shelled shrimps
100 grams (0.22 lb) pork
20 grams (2/3 oz) lettuce
3 grams (1/2 tsp) salt
1 1/2 grams (1/3 tsp) MSG
500 grams (1 cup) water

Directions：
1. Crush the bean curd to make a mash.

2. Grind the shrimps and pork. Add the 1 g (1/6 tsp) of salt and 1/2 g (1/8 tsp) MSG to each and mix until each becomes sticky.

3. Put 40 g (1 1/3 oz) mashed bean curd evenly on a piece of gauze cloth. Add 20 g (2/3 oz) respectively of shrimp and pork, fold the cloth to make a dumpling shape. Repeat the same process to make a total of 8 to 10 dumplings out of the total ingredients prepared. Steam them until they are done.

4. Put the bean curd dumplings in boiling water. Add the remaining salt and MSG and put into serving bowls. Put some lettuce leaves around the inside of the bowl as dressing before serving.

Features：The food is in the shape of dumplings.
Taste：Simply delicious.

酿豆腐

主料：豆腐 400 克

辅料：火腿 20 克、香菇 10 克、罐装笋 10 克、葱末 5 克

调料：盐 2 克、味精 1 克、油 5 克、湿淀粉 5 克、料酒 5 克

制作：①火腿用水煮熟，冷却后切成末，香菇、笋分别洗净切成末。

②将豆腐切成 5 厘米长、3.5 厘米宽、2.5 厘米厚的长方形，然后用小刀将豆腐雕成"凹"状（状似一只无盖的盒子），排列放在盘中，里面放火腿末、香菇末、笋末、葱末，再撒上盐、味精，淋上料酒和油，上笼蒸 5 分钟取出。

③炒锅烧热，倒入蒸豆腐时渗出的汤烧沸，用湿淀粉勾芡，均匀浇在豆腐上即可。

特点：造型独特，口感滑嫩

口味：咸鲜

Steamed Tasty Bean Curd

Ingredients：

400 grams (0.88 lb) bean curd
20 grams (2/3 oz) ham
10 grams (1/3 oz) mushrooms
10 grams (1/3 oz) canned bamboo shoots
5 grams (1/6 oz) finely cut scallions
2 grams (1/3 tsp) salt
1 gram (1/4 tsp) MSG
5 grams (1 tsp) cooking oil
5 grams (1 tsp) mixture of cornstarch and water
5 grams (1 tsp) cooking wine

Directions：

1. Boil the ham until it is done. When it has cooled off, cut it into fine dices. Also cut the mushrooms and bamboo shoots into fine dices.

2. Cut the bean curd into chunks of rectangular shape 5 cm (2 inches) long, 3.5cm (1.4 inches) wide and 2.5 cm (1 inch) thick. Cut hollows into the bean curd chunks (to make them like boxes without the top covers). Place the chunks on a plate. Fill the hollow parts with the ham, mushrooms, bamboo shoots, scallions, salt and MSG, and sprinkle on the cooking wine and oil. Steam for 5 minutes and take out.

3. Heat the wok, pour the juice from the steaming process into the wok. Thicken the sauce with the mixture of cornstarch and water and evenly sprinkle on the bean curd.

Features：Uniquely shaped and slippery to the bite.
Taste：Salty and delicious.

砂锅豆腐

主料：豆腐 400 克

辅料：火腿 20 克、罐装笋 10 克

调料：葱姜各 5 克、干红辣椒末 3 克、蚝油 8 克、盐 2 克、味精 1 克、色拉油 100 克、料酒 5 克、鸡汤 200 克

制作：①火腿用水煮熟，冷却后和笋一起分别切成 3 厘米长、2 厘米宽的片。

②将豆腐切成 3 厘米长、2 厘米宽、1.5 厘米厚的块。

③炒锅烧热，下油烧至八成热，分批下豆腐炸至表皮金黄，倒出沥油。

④原锅留油 5 克，下葱姜、干红辣椒爆出香味，倒入火腿片笋片略炒后，烹入料酒，下豆腐及鸡汤大火煮沸，放入盐、味精、蚝油调好口味，倒入砂锅中，改小火烧 10 分钟即可。

特点：味香汤浓

口味：鲜辣可口

Bean Curd in Earthen Pot

Ingredients：

400 grams (0.88 lb) bean curd
20 grams (2/3 oz) ham
10 grams (1/3 oz) canned bamboo shoots
5 grams (1/6 oz) ginger
5 grams (1/6 oz) scallions
3 grams (1/10 oz) chopped dried red chilies
8 grams (1 1/4 tsp) oyster sauce
2 grams (1/3 tsp) salt
1 gram (1/4 tsp) MSG
100 grams (7 tbsp) salad oil
5 grams (1 tsp) cooking wine
200 grams (2/5 cup) chicken soup

Directions：

1. Boil the ham until it is done. When it cools off, cut it, together with the bamboo shoots. into thin slices 3 cm (1.2 inches) long and 2 cm (0.8 inch) wide.

2. Cut the bean curd into chunks 3 cm (1.2 inches) long, 2 cm (0.8 inch) wide and 1.5 cm (0.6 inch) thick.

3. Heat the oil to 200-220℃ (390-430°F) and deep-fry the bean curd chunks batch by batch until they are golden yellow. Drain off the oil.

4. Keep 5 g (1 tsp) oil in the wok and stir-fry the scallions, ginger and dried red chilies till they pooduce a strong aroma. Add the sliced ham and bamboo shoots and stir-fry for a few seconds. Add the cooking wine, bean curd and chicken soup. Use a strong fire to bring it to a boil. Add the salt, MSG and oyster sauce. Pour into an earthen pot and simmer over low fire for 10 minutes.

Features：Richly flavored with a nice aroma.

Taste：Spicy and delicious.

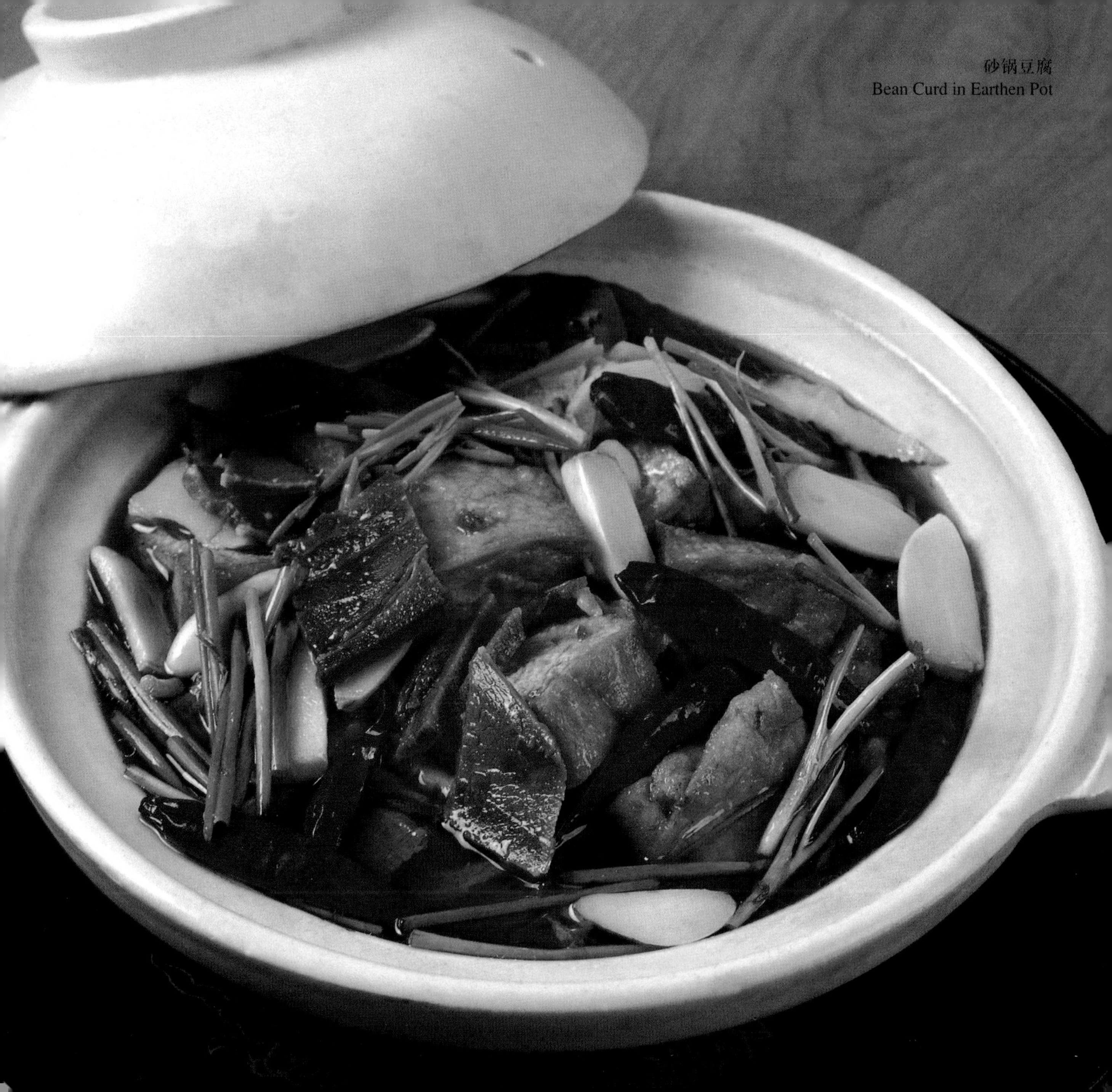

砂锅豆腐
Bean Curd in Earthen Pot

蟹粉豆腐

主料：豆腐 400 克，蟹 1 只约 250 克

调料：葱姜末各 5 克、盐 2 克、味精 1 克、胡椒粉 0.5 克、麻油 2 克、色拉油 50 克、香醋 5 克、料酒 5 克、鸡汤 150 克、湿淀粉 5 克

制作：①将蟹洗净上笼蒸熟，剥出蟹肉蟹黄弃除壳待用。②豆腐切成 1.5 厘米见方的丁，用沸水煮一下捞出，用清水漂清。

③炒锅烧热，下油加热至八成下葱姜爆出香味，倒入蟹肉，略炒，烹入料酒，放入香醋，倒入鸡汤煮沸后放入豆腐丁，下盐、味精改小火烧 5 分钟，用湿淀粉勾芡，出锅装盘淋上麻油，撒上胡椒粉即可。

特点：色泽金黄

口味：鲜嫩爽滑，香味浓郁

Bean Curd with Crab Meat

Ingredients：
400 grams (0.88 lb) bean curd
1 crab weighing about 250 grams (0.55 lb)
5 grams (1/6 oz) finely cut scallions
5 grams (1/6 oz) chopped ginger
2 grams (1/3 tsp) salt
1 gram (1/4 tsp) MSG
1/2 gram (1/10 tsp) pepper powder
2 grams (2/5 tsp) sesame oil
5 grams (1 tsp) vinegar
5 grams (1 tsp) cooking wine
50 grams (3 1/2 tbsp) salad oil
150 grams (1/3 cup) chicken soup
5 grams (1 tsp) mixture of cornstarch and water

Directions：
1. Wash and steam the crab until it is done. Take out the crab meat (both the white and reddish parts). Get rid of the shell.

2. Cut the bean curd into dices 1.5 cm ((0.6 inch) long on each side. Quick-boil in water and then run through cold water to wash clean.

3. Heat the oil in a wok to 200-220℃ (390-430˚F) and stir-fry the scallions and ginger until they produce a distinctive aroma. Add the crab meat and quickly stir several times. Add the cooking wine, vinegar and chicken soup and bring to a boil. Add the bean curd, salt and MSG, and cook for 5 minutes over a low fire. Thicken the sauce with the mixture of cornstarch and water. Sprinkle on the sesame oil and take out to serve.

Features：Nicely looking with shiny yellowish color.
Taste：Refreshing, tasty and succulent.

蟹粉豆腐
Bean Curd with Crab Meat

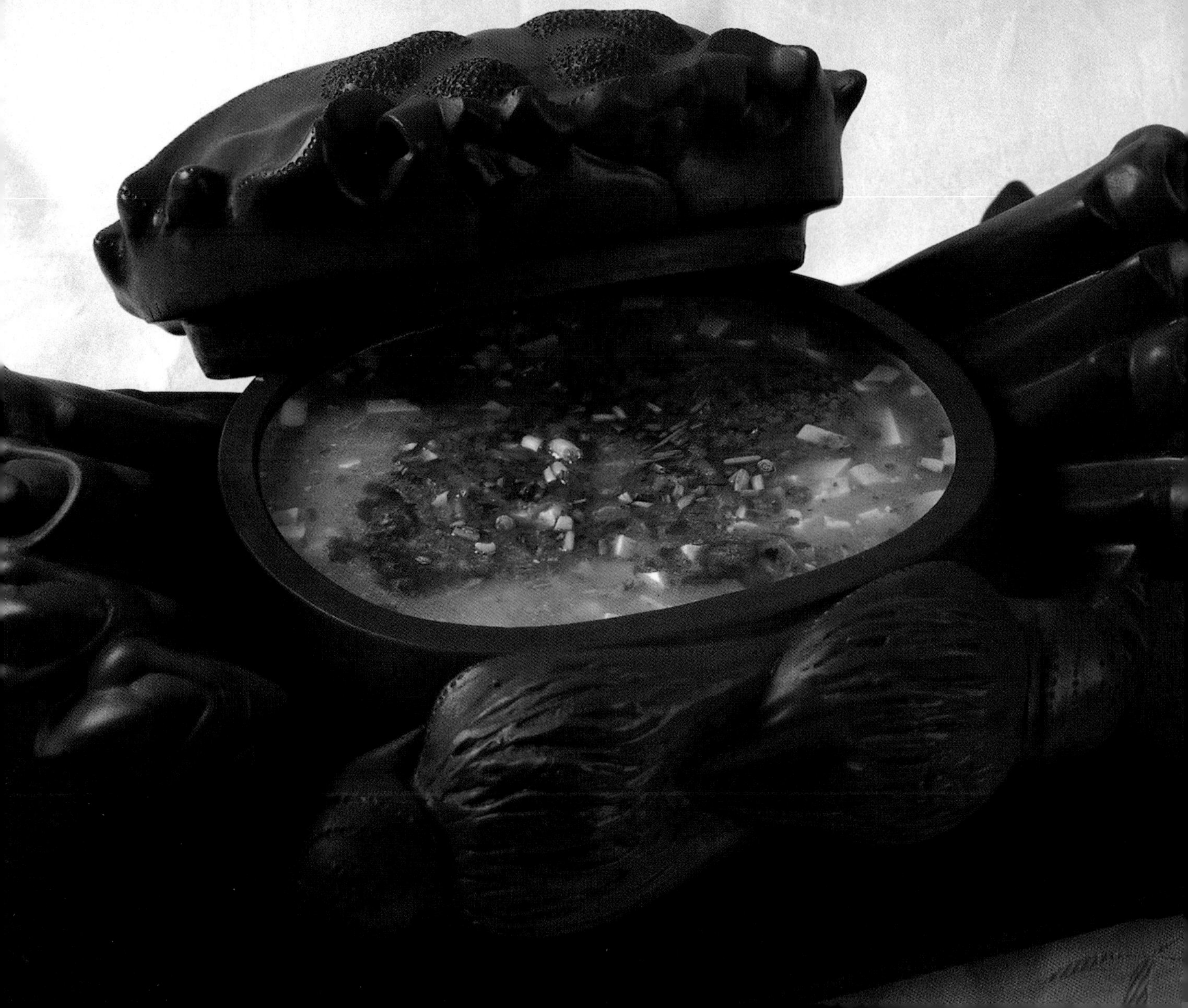

五香豆腐干

主料：方豆腐干16块（约250克）

调料：味精1克、酱油20克、糖5克、鸡汤150克、五香粉5克、色拉油25克

制作：①方豆腐干用沸水煮一下，再用清水漂清待用。②炒锅烧热至五成，下鸡汤、五香粉、酱油煮沸，然后放入方豆腐干、味精、糖大火煮5分钟，再改小火烧20分钟，收干汤汁，淋油出锅装盘。

特点：色呈酱红，油亮润泽

口味：鲜香

Five-flavored Bean Curd Cheese

Ingredients：
16 pieces (about 250 grams or 0.55 lb) bean curd cheese
1 gram (1/4 tsp) MSG
20 grams (1 tbsp) soy sauce
5 grams (1 tsp) sugar
150 grams (11 tbsp) chicken soup
5 grams (1 tsp) five-flavored powder
25 grams (1 2/3 tbsp) salad oil

Directions：
1. Boil the bean curd cheese in water and then run through cold water to wash it clean.

2. Heat the oil in a wok to 110-135℃ (230-275˚F). Add the chicken soup, five-flavored powder and soy sauce and bring to a boil. Put in the pieces of bean curd cheese, MSG and sugar, and bring to a boil over a strong fire letting it cook for 5 minutes. Turn to a low fire to continue to cook for 20 minutes. Use a strong fire to boil off some of the soup. Sprinkle on the oil and serve.

Features：Shiny in brownish red color.
Taste：Simply delicious.

五香豆腐干
Five-flavored Bean Cheese

三层豆腐

主料：豆腐 400 克

辅料：火腿 300 克

调料：盐 2 克、味精 2 克、湿淀粉 5 克、色拉油 25 克

制作：①将豆腐切成 6 厘米见方、1 厘米厚的片。

②火腿用水煮熟，切成末待用。

③在豆腐片的一面撒上盐、味精、火腿末，然后在其上叠放一片豆腐，再在豆腐上撒上味精、火腿末，再在上面叠放一片豆腐。然后对角切二刀，一分为四，上笼蒸熟（约 10 分钟）取出。

④炒锅烧热至五成，倒入蒸豆腐时渗出的汤汁，用湿淀粉勾芡烧沸，浇在豆腐上即可。

特点：色白

口味：鲜嫩

Three-level Bean Curd

Ingredients：
400 grams (0.88 lb) bean curd
300 grams (0.66 lb) ham
2 grams (1/3 tsp) salt
2 grams (1/2 tsp) MSG
5 grams (1 tsp) mixture of cornstarch and water
25 grams (1 2/3 tbsp) salad oil

Directions：
1. Cut the bean curd into slices 6 cm (2.4 inches) long and 1 cm (0.4 inch) thick.

2. Boil the ham until it is done. Cut and chop it into crumbs.

3. Spread some salt, MSG and ham crumbs on one slice of bean curd, top it with another slice and again add salt, MSG and ham crumbs. Top it with another slice of bean curd. Now cut the bean curd sandwich twice from corner to corner to produce four diamond shapes. Place them in a container and steam until they are done.

4. Heat the oil in a wok to 110-135℃ (275-340˚F) and add the juice from steaming the bean curd. Thicken the sauce with the mixture of cornstarch and water, bring to a boil and sprinkle it on the dish.

Features：White in color.
Taste：Very delicious.

三层豆腐
Three-level Bean Curd

青椒干丝

主料：白豆腐干 150 克

辅料：青椒 75 克

调料：盐 1 克、味精 1 克、色拉油 15 克

制作：①将青椒洗净，去蒂、籽，切成丝。

②白豆腐干切成 6 厘米长、0.5 厘米粗的丝。

③将白豆腐干丝在沸水中煮 3 分钟捞起，再将青椒丝倒入沸水中烫一下，捞出沥干水分，放入盛干丝的盘中。

④在干丝、青椒中放入盐、味精，将炒锅烧热，下油烧至八成热，倒入干丝青椒中，均匀拌透即可。

特点：绿白相间，色泽悦目

口味：咸鲜爽口

Shredded Bean Cheese with Green Peppers

Ingredients：
150 grams (0.33 lb) bean curd cheese
75 grams (0.16 lb) green peppers
1 gram (1/6 tsp) salt
1 gram (1/4 tsp) MSG
15 grams (1 tbsp) salad oil

Directions：

1. Wash the green pepper clean. Remove the stems and seeds and cut into shreds.

2. Cut the bean curd cheese into shreds 6 cm (2.4 inches) long and 0.5 cm (0.2 inch) thick.

3. Boil the bean curd cheese shreds for 3 minutes and take out. Use the same water and quick-boil the shredded green peppers. Take out and drain off the water. Place both kinds of shreds on a plate.

4. Add salt and MSG on the shredded bean curd and green peppers. Heat the oil in a wok to 200-220℃ (390-430˚F) and sprinkle on the shredded ingredients. Mix well and the dish is ready.

Features：The combination of green and white colors makes an enticing dish.
Taste：Salty and refreshing.

青椒干丝
Shredded Bean Cheese with Green Peppers

小葱拌豆腐

主料：豆腐 400 克

辅料：榨菜 3 克、蒜 10 克

调料：熟油 20 克、辣油 10 克、盐 4 克、味精 1 克、葱末 10 克

制作：①将豆腐上笼蒸 2 分钟后，用清水漂清，放在盘中。榨菜、蒜洗净切成末。

②将熟油、辣油、盐、味精、葱末、榨菜末、蒜末，撒在豆腐上，吃时再拌匀。

特点：清爽可口

口味：咸香鲜嫩

Bean Curd Mixed with Tender Scallions

Ingredients：

400 grams (0.88 lb) bean curd

3 grams (1/10 oz) preserved salted mustard root

10 grams (1/3 oz) garlic

20 grams (1 1/2 tbsp) oil already cooked

10 grams (2 tsp) spicy oil

4 grams (2/3 tsp) salt

1 gram (1/4 tsp) MSG

10 grams (1/3 oz) scallions finely cut

Directions：

1. Steam the bean curd for 2 minutes and then run through cold water to wash it clean. Place it on a plate. Wash and chop the salted mustard root. Mash the garlic.

2. Sprinkle the cooked oil, spicy oil, salt, MSG, scallions, mustard root and mashed garlic on the bean curd. Mix only the moment before serving.

Features：Very refreshing and soothing to the mouth.
Taste：Salty and delicious.

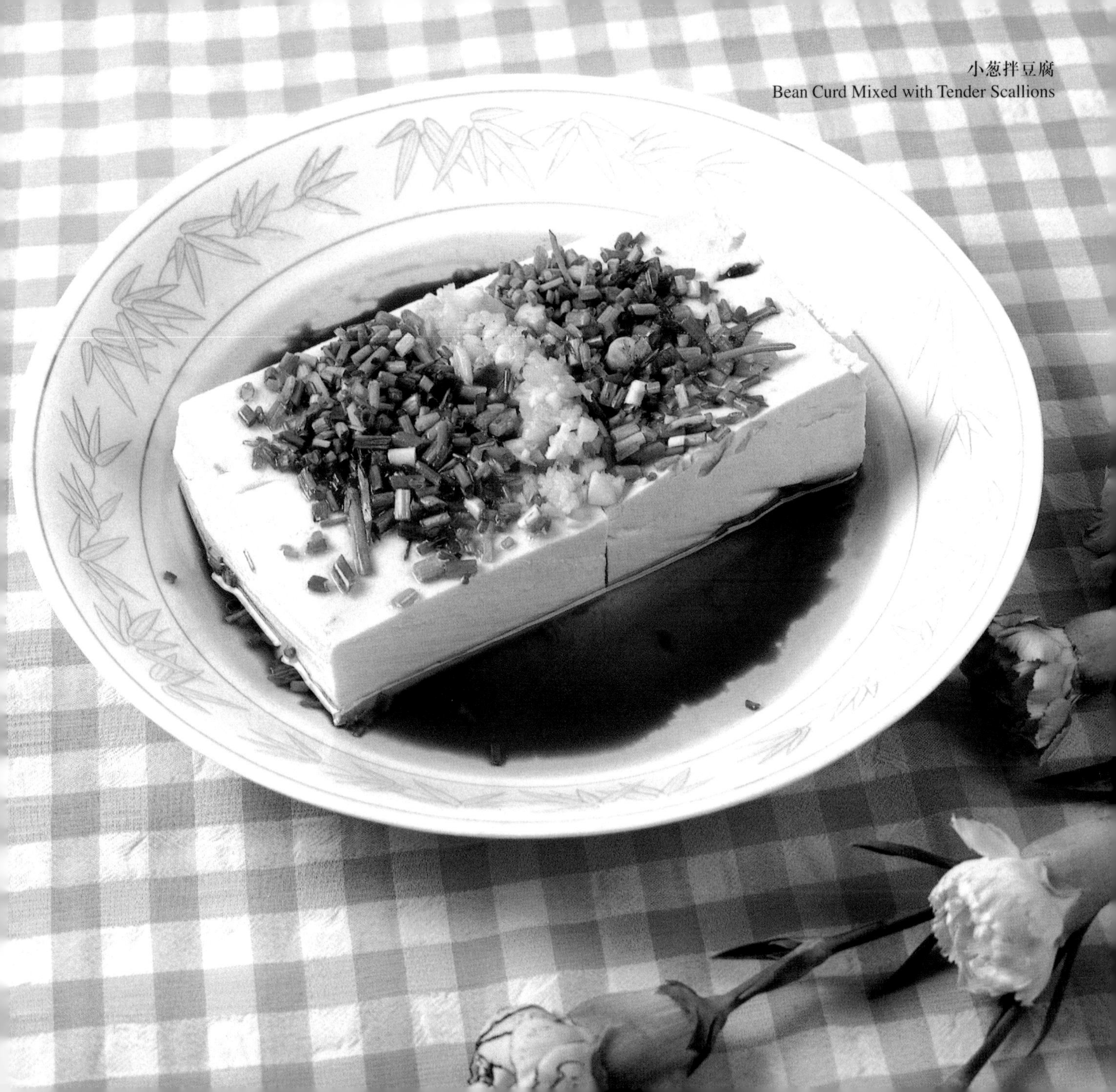

小葱拌豆腐
Bean Curd Mixed with Tender Scallions

计量换算表

1 磅	1 盎司	1 打兰	1 格令
约 454 克	约 28 克	约 1.8 克	约 0.06 克

调料 ml 勺	水	油	酱油	醋	料酒	盐	味精	砂糖	淀粉
1ml 勺	约 1 克	约 0.9 克	约 1.2 克	约 1 克	约 1 克	约 1.2 克	约 0.7 克	约 0.9 克	约 0.4 克
5ml 勺	约 5 克	约 4.5 克	约 6 克	约 5 克	约 5 克	约 6.3 克	约 3.7 克	约 4.5 克	约 2 克
15ml 勺	约 15 克	约 13.5 克	约 18 克	约 15 克	约 15 克	约 18.5 克	约 11 克	约 13 克	约 6 克
50ml 勺	约 50 克	约 55 克	约 60 克	约 50 克	约 50 克	约 63 克		约 42 克	约 20 克
500ml 勺	约 500 克	约 549 克	约 600 克	约 500 克	约 500 克	约 630 克			

A comparison of the weight systems

US system	1 grain(gr)	1ounce(oz)	1pound(lb)
Metric	0.065 gram(g)	28.35 grams(g)	454 grams(g)

A conversion table for measuring Chinese cooking ingredients*

ingredients cornstarch	water	ckg oil	soy sauce	vinegar	ckg wine	salt	MSG	sugar	cornstarch
1 pinch/1ml	1g	0.9g	1.2g	1g	1g	1.2g	0.7g	0.9g	0.4g
1tsp/5ml	5g	4.5g	6g	5g	5g	6.3g	3.7g	4.5g	2g
1tbsp/15ml	15g	13.5g	18g	15g	15g	18.5g	11g	13g	6g
1.76floz/50ml	50g	55g	60g	50g	50g	63g		42g	20g
3.52floz/1cup	500g	549g	600g	500g	500g	630g			

*All figures in grams given here are approximate as the exact equivalents will result in too many digits after the decimal point.

在编辑《学做中国菜》系列丛书的过程中，得到了苏州饭店的大力支持和帮助。作为苏州市旅游业的骨干企业苏州饭店已有数十年的历史，饭店拥有一流的烹饪厨师，经验丰富，技艺精湛。今借此书出版之机，我们对苏州饭店给予的支持，深表感谢!

We wish to thank the Suzhou Hotel, which kindly provided strong support and assistance to the compilation of the *Learn to Cook Chinese Dishes* series. As a major tourist hotel in the city of Suzhou, the Suzhou Hotel has a history of dozens of years and is serviced by experienced first-class chefs.

图书在版编目（CIP）数据

学做中国菜·豆品类/《学做中国菜》编委会编．-北京：外文出版社，1999
ISBN 7-119-02489-2

Ⅰ．学… Ⅱ．学… Ⅲ．豆品类-烹饪-中国-汉、英对照 Ⅳ．TS972.1
中国版本图书馆 CIP 数据核字（1999）第 48185 号

Members of the Editorial Board:
    Sun Jiaping   Lu Qinpu
    Sun Shuming   Liu Chun'gen
    Lan Peijin
Dish preparation and text:
    Zhu Deming   Wen Jinshu
    Zhu Guifu   Zhang Guomin
    Zhang Guoxiang   Xu Rongming
    Cao Gang
Editor: Lan Peijin
English translation and editing:
    Huang Youyi   Foster Stockwell   Cong Guoling
Design: Lan Peijin
Photography: Sun Shuming   Liu Chun'gen   Lan Peijin
Cover design: Wang Zhi

编委：孙建平　鲁钦甫　孙树明
　　　刘春根　兰佩瑾
菜肴制作及撰文：朱德明　温金树
　　　　　　　　朱桂福　张国民
　　　　　　　　张国祥　徐荣明
　　　　　　　　曹　刚
责任编辑：兰佩瑾
英文翻译：黄友义　卓柯达　丛国玲
设计：兰佩瑾
摄影：孙树明　刘春根　兰佩瑾
封面设计：王　志

First Edition 2000

**Learn to Cook Chinese Dishes
—Bean Products**

ISBN 7-119-02489-2

©Foreign Languages Press
Published by Foreign Languages Press
24 Baiwanzhuang Road, Beijing 100037, China
Home Page：http://www.flp.com.cn
E-mail Addresses：info @ flp.com.cn
          sales @ flp.com.cn
Printed in the People's Republic of China

学做中国菜·豆品类

《学做中国菜》编委会　编

ⓒ　外文出版社
外文出版社出版
（中国北京百万庄大街 24 号）邮政编码 100037
外文出版社网页：http://www.flp.com.cn
外文出版社电子邮件地址：info @ flp.com.cn
          sales @ flp.com.cn
北京骏马行图文中心制版
天时印刷（深圳）有限公司印制
2000 年（24 开）第一版
2000 年第一版第一次印刷
（英汉）
ISBN 7-119-02489-2/J·1513（外）
08000（精）